INTERNATIONAL FINANCIAL REPORTING STANDARDS

Marlene Plumlee
The University of Utah

Prentice Hall

Boston Columbus Indianapolis New York San Francisco Upper Saddle River
Amsterdam Cape Town Dubai London Madrid Milan Munich Paris Montreal Toronto
Delhi Mexico City Sao Paulo Sydney Hong Kong Seoul Singapore Taipei Tokyo

Editor-in-Chief: Natalie Anderson
Acquisitions Editor: Julie Broich
Editorial Project Manager: Melissa Gill
Production Project Manager: Rhonda Aversa
Operations Specialist: Natacha Moore

Copyright © 2010 Pearson Education, Inc., publishing as Prentice Hall, One Lake Street, Upper Saddle River, New Jersey 07458. All rights reserved. Manufactured in the United States of America. This publication is protected by Copyright, and permission should be obtained from the publisher prior to any prohibited reproduction, storage in a retrieval system, or transmission in any form or by any means, electronic, mechanical, photocopying, recording, or likewise. To obtain permission(s) to use material from this work, please submit a written request to Pearson Education, Inc., Permissions Department, One Lake Street, Upper Saddle River, New Jersey 07458.

Many of the designations by manufacturers and seller to distinguish their products are claimed as trademarks. Where those designations appear in this book, and the publisher was aware of a trademark claim, the designations have been printed in initial caps or all caps.

Prentice Hall
is an imprint of

www.pearsonhighered.com

10 9 8 7 6 5 4 3 2 1
ISBN 13: 978-0-13-612304-0
ISBN 10: 0-13-612304-X

TABLE OF CONTENTS

Chapter 1 - INTERNATIONAL ACCOUNTING   Page 1

Chapter 2 - BACKGROUND AND SOME HISTORY   Page 11

Chapter 3 - CONCEPTUAL FRAMEWORKS   Page 26

Chapter 4 - US GAAP AND IFRS—AN EXAMPLE   Page 33

Chapter 5 - CATEGORIZING DIFFERENCES   Page 41

Chapter 6 - US GAAP AND IFRS—SOME DIFFERENCES   Page 52

ABOUT THE AUTHOR

Associate Professor Marlene A. Plumlee earned her PhD in Business Administration from the University of Michigan (1997) and has taught at the University of Utah since graduation. From August 2006 through July 2007 she served as an academic fellow for the Securities and Exchange Commission. During her time at the commission, Professor Plumlee worked in the Office of the Chief Accountant, working with both the Accounting and International Groups on various issues, including understanding the impact of International Financial Reporting Standards on the US capital markets, stock-option backdating, and the design of market-based measures for valuing employee stock options. She is a CPA and previously worked for Deloitte.

Professor Plumlee has taught a variety of course at the Undergraduate, Masters, and PhD levels, including Financial Accounting II, Financial Statement Analysis, and Current Issues in Accounting Research. She has designed and is currently teaching an upper-division International Accounting course. The course integrates International Financial Reporting Standards into a financial accounting course and leverages comparisons between US GAAP and IFRS to enhance the development of a "critical thinking" approach to financial accounting and reporting. The goal of the course and the related materials is to enhance student understanding of the links among the underlying transactions, the application of reporting standards for those transactions, and the financial reports obtained from a global/international perspective. Professor Plumlee's research examines the role of disclosure in explaining cross-firm differences in cost of capital and how attributes of information affect investors' use of that information. Her research has been published in the *Journal of Accounting Research, The Accounting Review, Accounting Horizons,* and the *Review of Accounting Studies.* She currently serves on the editorial board of *The Accounting Review* and reviews for a number of scholarly journals.

HOW TO USE THIS SUPPLEMENT

The supplement is broken into six chapters. The role of this supplement is to provide you with a framework to gain an understanding of IFRS and its potential impact on financial reporting. However, the issue of IFRS and its impact is more complex than can be covered in great detail in a supplement alone. Thus, throughout the supplement we provide Web addresses for the websites of the groups involved in this issue and specific topics of interest. We also provide discussion questions to encourage further analysis related to this issue.

Chapter 1 discusses the general context of accounting standards and two most widely used sets of standards in the world, i.e., US Generally Accepted Accounting Principles (US GAAP) and International Financial Reporting Standards (IFRS). If you are an accounting student or have a relatively strong understanding of accounting, you can probably skim this chapter or skip it entirely.

Chapter 2 provides background information about the use of US GAAP and IFRS as well as the 'players' that will ultimately affect how and when IFRS will be adopted internationally. Even with a good understanding of accounting, this section will probably be useful. It reinforces the three regulatory groups that affect accounting standards—accounting standard setters, security regulators, and audit regulators. It also provides a brief historical perspective of the use of US GAAP and IFRS.

Chapter 3 provides an overview of the conceptual frameworks that underlie the formation of US GAAP and IFRS. It also begins the discussions of how differences in conceptual frameworks or differences in the application of similar frameworks bring about differences in financial reports. In particular, differences in when specific transactions meet the criteria for recognition and in how assets and liabilities are measured are two sources of significant differences between US GAAP- and IFRS-generated financial reports. These two issues should be discussed and considered during the discussion of the conceptual frameworks. Chapter 5 includes a more detailed discussion of how recognition and measurement play into differences in both the values reported and the separation between balance sheet and income statement transactions.

Chapter 4 provides a brief comparison between two firms, one that employs US GAAP to prepare its financial reports (Monsanto) and one that employs IFRS to prepare its financial reports (Syngenta). It also discusses specific differences between IFRS and US GAAP reported income and stockholders' equity for Syngenta, based on a reconciliation between these two amounts prepared by the firm to comply with SEC reporting requirements. This discussion provides students with an example of how reported values differ between the two sets of standards applied for a specific firm. The discussion focuses on the source of the reported differences (e.g., recognition, measurement), to provide a broader perspective than focusing on the specific differences (e.g., pensions, mergers). In addition, this chapter provides general information regarding reported differences between US GAAP and IFRS, in terms of the magnitude and sign of those differences across the set of companies that filed 20-Fs with the SEC during 2006. This information is useful in understanding how reporting under IFRS might impact US firms currently using US GAAP.

The 20-F reconciliations provide a source of salient examples where US GAAP and IFRS reporting produce materially different results in reported values. As such, they have the potential to improve our understanding of those differences. In addition to presenting the monetary differences in the reported numbers based on IFRS and US GAAP, the reconciliation footnotes include detailed discussions of the difference in the transaction(s) that causes the reported differences. These discussions can be very useful in better understanding the technical differences between US GAAP and IFRS in specific situations.

Chapter 5 presents a system for classifying differences in both reported outcomes and sources of differences between US GAAP and IFRS. Most discussions of differences between US GAAP and IFRS focus on specific accounts (e.g., intangible assets, inventory) and describe technical differences in how specific transactions related to those accounts differ between US GAAP and IFRS. In this supplement we present a broader perspective by categorizing differences based on how the reported outcomes differ and the sources of those differences. The purpose of this categorization is to provide a mechanism for better understanding how to interpret and consider differences between US GAAP and IFRS than simply viewing technical differences alone. This section includes a detailed discussion of a specific difference between IFRS and US GAAP reported by Syngenta using these dichotomies and factors.

Chapter 6 discusses several sources of significant differences between US GAAP and IFRS reported values, using the system detailed in Chapter 5. This material links your understanding of why differences exist with the broader perspective of where differences appear in reported outcomes. Your increased understanding of the source of these differences will assist in understanding the potential effects on financial reporting of the SEC adopting IFRS for use by US firms. In addition, understanding the sources of differences along with a knowledge of primary sources of material differences will assist in comparing firms based on US GAAP financial reports with firms based on IFRS financial reports.

CHAPTER 1
INTERNATIONAL ACCOUNTING

This chapter provides an overview of the current business environment that has influenced the development and application of the two most commonly used sets of accounting standards in the world: US Generally Accepted Accounting Principles (US GAAP) and International Financial Reporting Standards (IFRS). It includes a description of the context that surrounds the past and continued development and application of these two sets of standards throughout the world and a discussion of both harmonization (a means of improving comparability across sets of standards by setting limits on the alternatives allowed within each set) and convergence (where the two sets of standards are aligned and ultimately replaced by a single set) of accounting standards.

THE ROLE OF ACCOUNTING

Accounting can be defined as an information system that translates economic activities of businesses into financial reports useful to stakeholders as they make decisions about that business. Accounting systems are designed to gather and process financial data in such a way to allow interested individuals an understanding of the past and expected future performance of a business entity, a firm. These systems generate values provided in financial reports. Firms that receive funding from investors and creditors have an obligation to keep those investors and creditors informed about their financial performance, condition, and prospects. In addition, these firms are generally accountable to others who may directly or indirectly provide resources, including employees, governments, and the community within which they operate. The role of accounting itself is to collect and process data in such a way as to provide the information needed to enhance users' abilities to make informed, superior decisions.

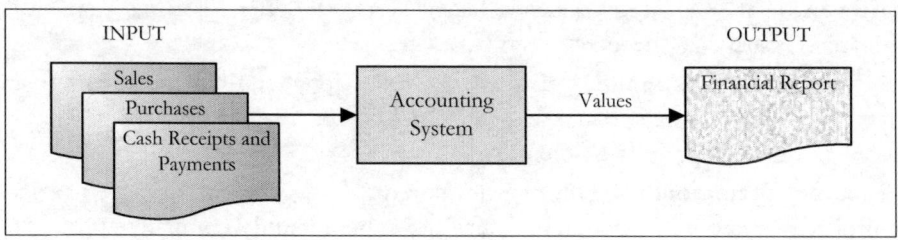

In this supplement, we focus on financial reports prepared for a broad community of external stakeholders, which includes creditors, investors, suppliers, and employees. The financial reports are based on the two sets of standards most commonly employed by firms throughout the world: US GAAP and IFRS. The Financial Accounting Standards Board (FASB) establishes US GAAP standards, while IFRS is the set of accounting standards established by the International Accounting Standards Board (IASB).

US GAAP and IFRS both include four statements, (an income statement, balance sheet, statement of cash flows, and statement of stockholders' equity) in a complete set of financial statements. In addition to information collected and stated in monetary terms (e.g., dollars or euros) within these four statements, footnote disclosures are included as a fundamental component of a complete set of financial statements. These disclosures present a wealth of financial information that may be of considerable interest to stakeholders that may not be effectively communicated using numeric values alone. These detailed disclosures provide financial related information to supplement and/or augment the discrete information included in the statements themselves. Footnote disclosures may include information that assists financial statement users in understanding how a company calculates the values presented (e.g., how it calculates its tax expense or pension expense), the underlying assumptions that a company makes in estimating a value (e.g., assumptions used to estimate a pension liability or stock option expense), or general information about various issues (e.g., information about its competitors and risks that it faces). These disclosures provide contextual information that is key to enhancing users' abilities to understand more fully the economics that underlie the numbers themselves.

FINANCIAL STATEMENTS
Balance Sheet – One of four required statements that presents the assets, debts, and stockholders' equity as of a specific date.
Cash Flow Statement – One of four required statements that presents how a firm has obtained/used its funds (cash) across a period of time. Captures changes in balance sheets between two dates.
Statement of Stockholders' Equity – One of four required statements that presents the elements that make up stockholders equity and the changes therein during a period of time.
Income Statement – One of four required statements that presents information about the accrual revenues and expenses and a company's profit or loss over a period of time.
Footnote Disclosures – Provide financial related information to supplement and/or argument the discrete information included in the financial statements.

The Objectives of Financial Reporting

Financial reporting is the principal mechanism by which firms report the results of their economic activities to stakeholders. In our discussions we will consider the purpose of financial reporting in broad terms as well as how the various perspectives and objectives of financial reporting affect the accounting standards. Stakeholders' interests in a company and its profitability are a function of their perspectives. Consider differences in perspectives between an individual who makes an investment in a company's stock versus one who buys a company's bonds. A stockholder wins or loses along with the company as a whole, which leads to an interest in the company's profitability. However, a bondholder benefits when a company makes principal and interest payments, which leads to an interest in the company's current cash flows and ability to repay debts. Meeting the need of one user may not meet the needs of others. Standards selected often reflect the perspectives of standard setters, who must choose among different standards based on which one they believe will provide the most generally useful information.

Ultimately, the objectives of financial reporting (which may be influenced by various perspectives) are integral in understanding how accounting standards are developed and established. In considering the 'most appropriate' means of accounting for economic transactions, standard setters must take into account the objectives of financial reporting. From a broad perspective, there are a large number of 'reporting objectives' that might be considered. For example, potential objectives of financial reporting include:

- To provide information useful to both present and potential investors in making rational investment decisions;
- To provide information useful to creditors and employees in making rational credit and other decisions;
- To provide information that helps stakeholders assess the amounts, timing, and uncertainty about future cash flows;
- To provide information about the economic resources of an firm and claims on those resources and the effects of transactions, events, and circumstances that change its resources;
- To conform to regulatory requirements (including income and other tax authorities).

In discussing the role of accounting standards, it is necessary to consider the sometimes competing objectives of financial reporting and how those objectives might influence the selection of the 'best' accounting standard for recording a set of economic transactions. In a world with multiple sets of accounting standards, it is also essential to consider differences across countries and time in determining whose perspective is considered the most important in setting standards.

The Role of Accounting Standards

Much of the discussion in this course will center on the development and application of accounting standards and their ability to capture and cumulate economic transactions so that interested and educated users understand the effect of those transactions on the overall financial health of a reporting entity, which we will refer to as a firm. In these discussions it is essential to understand both what constitutes a set of accounting standards and the role of accounting standards in the translation of economic activity into financial reports.

Accounting standards are effectively a 'users manual,' which provides varying levels of detail to individuals responsible for preparing financial reports (preparers) (e.g., managers and auditors) in how to record business transactions. Ultimately, recording these transactions translates a firm's financial performance into a set of coherent and concise financial statements. The end result of applying those accounting standards to a firm's transactions is information that will be used to formulate a set of financial statements.

The role of accounting standards is twofold—to provide structure to managers and preparers as they decide how to record a given transaction or a set of similar transactions and to provide stakeholders with an understanding of the links between the reported amounts and the economic transactions that underlie them. Firms across the world prepare financial statements with a similar overall objective—to provide information to stakeholders. However, as discussed earlier, *accounting standards* established within various countries and across time often differ in how they account for the same economic event. The core and crux of this supplement is the differing perspectives, objectives, and theoretic underpinnings between US GAAP and IFRS that ultimately result in the same economic activity being recorded to obtain different values in the recorded outcome due *solely* to the set of accounting standards employed.

Differences in accounting standards exist across countries for a variety of reasons. They may be due to differences across the local environments in which the reporting firm operates including the:

- Operation of legal systems (e.g., litigation and other factors);
- Political systems (e.g., the degree of central government control);
- Type and scale of economic activity;
- Effect of international influences and openness of an economy;
- Corporate governance (the exercise of power over and responsibility for a firm's structures and practices);
- Stability of the economy and inflation rates.

In addition, in some countries, financial reports prepared using these accounting standards may be used for statutory reporting purposes without modification, which provides differing incentives to standard setters. Particularly within a world with increasing globalization of trade, however, there exists substantial pressure from all stakeholders to improve comparability across firms. Simply put, it has become less acceptable to report the same transactions in different ways solely due to where the transaction is recorded.

An Example: Different Outcomes

The key issue to appreciate throughout the discussion of the two sets of standards is that the application of each set of standards to the *same* economic activities will, in many cases, result in *different* reported financial statements. How can two sets of accounting standards take the same economic event and report different outcomes? A relatively simple example demonstrates how this might happen and highlights what effects it might have.

Consider a transaction where a company decides to invest in research to modify automobile engines in order to produce kits that, once installed, result in a significant increase in their mileage rate. The company hires an individual who is skilled in modifying engines and has a design for a 'kit' that could be installed in cars built between 1998–2006 that will allow them to improve their overall mileage by 20%. However, there is still work to be done before the product can be sold. In technical terms, "technical and commercial feasibility of the asset for sale or use have been established." How should the company account for the transactions—where it pays an individual to work on a product that will eventually be sold to produce income? The FASB has determined that the costs associated with the activity do not meet the standard it has established under US GAAP to qualify as an asset, while the IASB has determined that those same costs do meet the standard *it* has established under IFRS. Both the FASB and the IASB understand that there is uncertainty regarding whether the development costs will produce an *economic* asset. However, they have come down on different sides of the issue. Both the FASB and IASB have very similar definitions of what constitutes an asset (which we discuss in Chapter 3). However, in this specific setting, their respective judgments differ.

So, what is the difference in the financial reports produced under US GAAP and IFRS? The simplified example below demonstrates how the balance sheet and income statement would differ when US GAAP expenses the cost ($750) in the year the expenditure is made, while IFRS capitalizes and then amortizes the cost over three years. A firm is formed in 2004 with $2000 of cash and no liabilities. The only transactions are in cash—the company pays $750 for development in 2005 then begins selling the car kits in 2006. Under US GAAP, the development costs reduce reported income in the year the cash outlay occurs, while under IFRS those same costs are capitalized to produce an asset in that year that will be expensed in future periods. As demonstrated below, the reported income and assets differ between US GAAP and IFRS across the year the expenditure is made as well as all future periods until the asset is fully amortized.

Thus, a firm that applies US GAAP would have lower reported income and fewer reported assets in the year of the cash outlay than a firm that applied IFRS. In subsequent years, a firm that applies US GAAP would have higher reported income and fewer reported assets than a firm that applies IFRS, until the IFRS asset is fully depreciated. These reported differences would obtain, although we know that, from an economic perspective, *economic* income and assets are unaffected by the reporting differences.

Expensing (US GAAP) vs. Capitalizing (IFRS)

US GAAP Standards

	0	0	0	0	0
Cash	2000	1250	2250	3500	5000
Car Kit		0	0	0	0
Total Assets	0	0	0	0	0
Equity	2000	2000	2000	2000	2000
Prior Year RE			(750)	250	1500
Current Year NI		(750)	1000	1250	1500
Total Eqity	0	0	0	0	0
Revenue		0	1000	1250	1500
Expense		750	0	0	0
Net Income (Loss)		0	0	0	0

IFRS Standards

	0	0	0	0	0
Cash	2000	1250	2250	3500	5000
Car Kit		750	500	250	0
Total Assets	0	0	0	0	0
Equity	2000	2000	2000	2000	2000
Prior Year RE			0	750	1750
Current Year NI		0	750	1000	1250
Total Eqity	0	0	0	0	0
Revenue		0	1000	1250	1500
Expense		0	250	250	250
Net Income (Loss)		0	0	0	0

FINANCIAL REPORTING CONTEXT

In the US, publicly traded firms are required to apply the set of accounting standards developed and adopted by the FASB, US GAAP, in their financial reports filed with the US Securities and Exchange Commission (SEC)[1]. Prior to the 1990s, many considered US GAAP the 'gold standard' in terms of financial reporting in that the application of these standards provided more 'transparent, high-quality' financial reports than the application of other sets of standards. Transparent and high-quality financial reports are defined as financial reports that more clearly capture the economics, are more easily understood, and more consistently record similar transactions across time than less transparent and lower-quality financial reports

Prior to the 1990s, accounting standards were developed and adopted by interested parties (e.g., the Accounting Standards Board in the United Kingdom (UK) and the French Conseil Nationale de la Comptabilité in France) for use within their own jurisdictions. Each country would set standards for use within that country, and security market regulatory organizations within those jurisdictions would require that firms apply their specified set of standards. (E.g., firms that were listed on the UK securities market (the London Stock Exchange) were required to apply UK GAAP in financial statements filed with them.) As long as markets were relatively 'closed' to individuals outside a given jurisdiction, this system of a separate set of standards for each jurisdiction was relatively efficient. However, in a world with minimal borders, particularly in terms of capital formation and trade, there is less tolerance for differences in accounting standards that mandate that two firms with identical economic activities provide financial reports with different values in terms of profitability and financial position (as demonstrated above). Consequently, over the last decade there has been a concerted effort by standard setters and regulators throughout the world to focus on establishing a single set of accounting standards, which provide financial reports that are not influenced by the jurisdiction where the transactions are recorded and reported.

Standard setters and regulators within the major economic powers (including Germany, Japan, the UK, and the US) are on the forefront of working toward the establishment of a single set of international accounting standards. While it might be possible for multiple sets of standards to produce equally high-quality, transparent financial reports, as long as there are differences across those sets of standards, comparability across firms that apply different sets of standards is limited by the accounting standards. The international community's efforts to

---

[1] Chapter 2 includes a discussion of the security market regulators and other groups mentioned in this section (e.g., SEC and IOSCO). Please refer to that section for a detailed description of those groups and their role in the adoption of IFRS.

move towards standards that provide comparable statements across jurisdictions can be described by one of two methods: harmonization and convergence. While the end result of the two is the same, the process by which it is accomplished differs. Harmonization accommodates national differences in the process by working to improve comparability by reducing the options available within various sets of standards. Convergence suggests making changes within each set of standards such that they will converge to a common outcome—a single set of standards used by all. Initially, the process employed by the FASB and IASB could be best described as harmonization between US GAAP and IFRS. Across time, however, the agenda has changed from harmonization to convergence.

Currently, the FASB and the IASB and their interpretative bodies are working together to eliminate differences between US GAAP and IFRS in similar standards and in their interpretation and application. The FASB and the IASB have formally announced their mutual commitments to the convergence of US GAAP and IFRS. Joint projects are currently being conducted related to various technical issues as well as a project to establish a single conceptual framework agreed to by both boards. Topics that will increase convergence currently receive priority placement on the boards' agendas.

While many suggested that US GAAP would and should emerge as the internationally accepted set of standards, others suggested that the set of international standards should come about through a selection of the 'best' standards across a variety of GAAPs. Still others believed that the best means of providing the international standards would be to start from scratch. IFRS has come about as a combination of the three—some of it is very similar to US GAAP, some IFRSs reflect the proposed 'best' method of accounting for transactions taken from a variety of GAAPs, and some standards have been produced independently.

There are more than eighty countries that currently *require* the use of IFRS for the preparation of financial statements of some, or all, of their domestic listed firms. At least another twenty countries *permit* the use of IFRS. In addition, there are a number of other countries that are pursuing a formal policy of convergence with IFRS. By 2005 the European Union, Australia, Hong Kong, and South Africa had all adopted IFRS, while Japan and the United States were working closely with the IASB to converge their standards. In 2007 the Accounting Standards Board of Japan agreed to work with the IASB to eliminate major differences between IFRS and Japanese GAAP by 2008. Canada, once on a path to converge with US GAAP, is now mandating the use of IFRS by January 1, 2011. In a recent 'proposing release' (in November 2008), the SEC outlined a roadmap to the adoption of IFRS by US public companies, which proposed allowing some US firms to use IFRS as early as 2009 and a mandatory transition for all firms beginning in 2014.

SEC Factors to Consider Before Adoption
(1) Improvements in accounting standards. (2) Increased accountability and funding of the IASCF/IASB to ensure independence. (3) Improvement in the ability to use XBRL for reporting. (4) Education and training in the US related to IFRS.

While most agree that the adoption of a single set of standards will increase the comparability and improve the efficiency of the markets, it is important to consider factors that may affect the positive impacts of a single set of internationally accepted accounting standards. Ultimately, even if there exists a single set of transparent, high-quality accounting standards available to all, there are still reasons why this may not lead to international harmonization of the financial reports. These reasons include:

- Less than 'full' adoption of the accounting standards;
- Inconsistent application of the accounting standards;
- Inconsistent regulatory oversight of the financial reports;
- Cultural differences in similar economic transactions.

CONCLUSION

Financial reports generated through accounting systems based on a set of accounting standards are designed to provide users with information regarding the underlying economic activities of a given firm. Users may infer that differences in the outcomes in financial reports reflect differences in the economic activities completed. However, financial reports generated using different sets of accounting standards will result in different outcomes due *solely* to the set of accounting standards employed. In response to concerns from stakeholders regarding the role of accounting standards in reported outcomes, there have been substantial changes in financial reporting standards throughout the world. Over the next decade, it is very plausible that US corporations will no longer be allowed to use US GAAP but instead will be required to apply IFRS in financial reporting. In addition to being aware of specific differences in reported outcomes between US GAAP and IFRS, understanding why these two sets of standards differ and the expected impact of applying IFRS rather than US GAAP is important as we move forward toward a more international economy.

Pause and Reflect: *The FASB and IASB have a number of joint projects they are currently working on as a means of converging to a single set of global accounting standards. Use the links provided and other sources to determine what joint projects are currently in process and the status of those projects. Consider the importance of these various projects (how broad are the differences that currently exist and the topics themselves) and the current status of them to assess the overall status of convergence between US GAAP and IFRS. In addition, consider the ongoing projects of each board that are in process but are not considered joint projects. In your analysis, make use of more detailed and current information about the projects and concerns raised by various parties.*

Resources:
FASB website – http://www.fasb.org/
FASB projects – http://www.fasb.org/project/
IASB website – http://www.iasb.org/Home.htm
IASB projects –
http://www.iasb.org/Current+Projects/IASB+Projects/IASB+Work+Plan.htm
Some joint projects:
Overall –
Conceptual frameworks –
http://www.fasb.org/project/conceptual_framework.shtml
Financial statement presentation –
http://www.fasb.org/project/financial_statement_presentation.shtml
Revenue recognition –
http://www.fasb.org/project/revenue_recognition.shtml
Lease accounting –
http://www.fasb.org/project/leases.shtml

CHAPTER 2
BACKROUND AND SOME HISTORY

This section begins with a discussion of the three sets of 'players' in the setting and application of accounting standards: accounting standard setters, security market regulators, and audit standard setters/regulators. These groups are key to the process of adopting and enforcing accounting standards internationally and the ability of any set of standards to generate consistent financial reports. We also provide a historical perspective on the development of accounting standards as well as the standard-setting process over the last decades and a brief description of context that surrounds the past and continued development, harmonization, and application of US GAAP or IFRS.

THE PLAYERS

Before discussing the processes that have generated the current state of accounting standards, it is essential to have an understanding of the various groups involved in the standard-setting process, including the application of accounting standards. The three main groups we will discuss are accounting standard setters, security market regulators, and auditors and audit regulators.

Accounting Standard Setters

The FASB, established in 1973, is the private firm that the SEC has charged with setting US accounting standards—US GAAP. The Financial Accounting Foundation (FAF) is a nonprofit foundation that selects the FASB members and oversees its professional activities. The FAF board of trustees, comprised of members from eight groups that represent a broad cross-section of individuals interested in the preparation and/or use of financial reports (i.e., the American Accounting Association; American Institute of Certified Public Accountants; Association for Investment Management and Research; Financial Executives International; Government Finance Officers Association; Institute of Management Accountants; National Association of State Auditors, Comptrollers, and Treasurers; and the Securities Industry Association), nominate FASB board members. The FAF also appoints the Financial Accounting Standards Advisory Committee (FASAC), which consults with and provides independent advice to the FASB on major policy and technical issues.

    The current FASB includes five full-time accounting standard setters (down from seven as of July 2008), a supporting staff, and significant advisory support. Four of the five board members are CPAs, two were partners at a 'Big Four' accounting firm, two were in industry, and one was an academic. (The Big Four are the four largest international accounting firms (PricewaterhouseCoopers, Deloitte, Ernst & Young, and KPMG), which handle the vast majority of audits for publicly traded companies as well as many private companies. Based on the most recent data, these four firms have gross revenues in excess of a trillion dollars and employ over five hundred thousand.) Two additional groups established by the FASB, the former Standing Interpretations Committee (SIC) and the Emerging Issues Task Force (EITF), provide specific assistance to the Board in applying and developing standards. The SIC focused on providing more detailed guidance than what might be found in an accounting standard. The EITF was formed to assist the FASB by addressing narrow implementation, application, or other emerging issues that can be analyzed within existing GAAP. Members include auditors, preparers, and users of financial statements who work to reach consensus on how to account for new and emerging issues in the rapidly changing business environment.

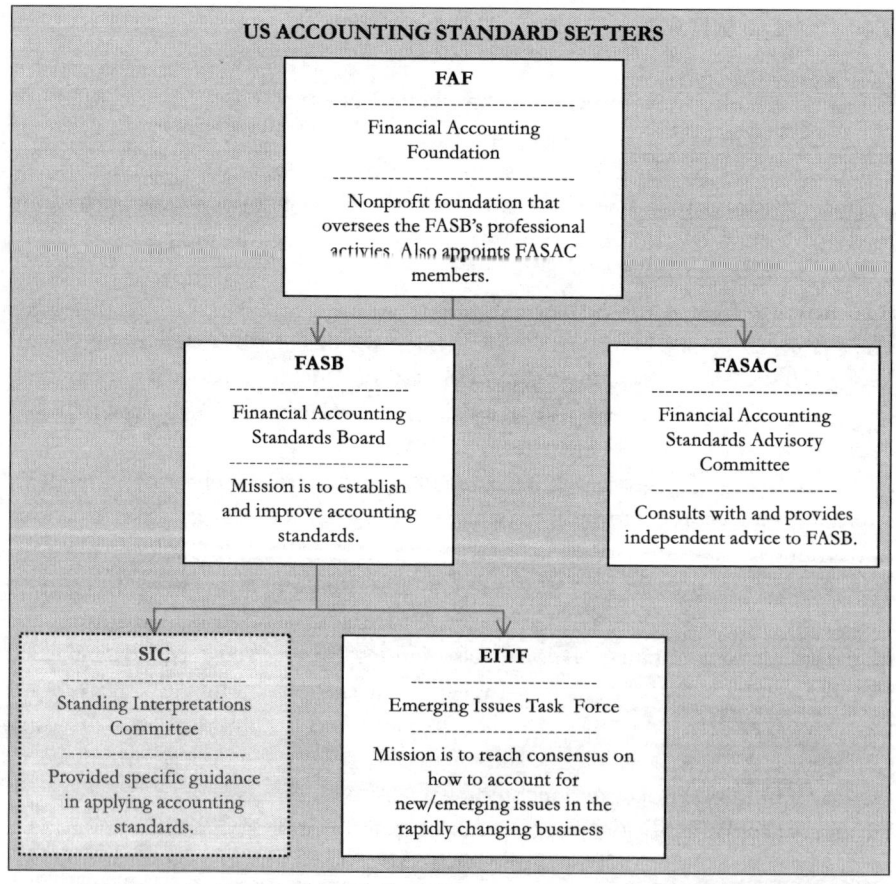

The structure of the IFRS standard-setting process was modeled after the US system and is similar in many ways. The current IFRS accounting standard setter is the IASB, established in 2001. The International Accounting Standards Committee Foundation (IASCF), an independent organization with 22 trustees, appoints IASB board members, oversees the work of the IASB, and provides fundraising to support international standard setting. The IASCF trustees are drawn from a variety of professional backgrounds and broad cross-section of the international community—six each from North America, Europe, and Asia/Australia/New Zealand areas and the remaining four from the rest of the world to try to establish geographical balance. The IASB also has an advisory board, the Standards Advisory Council (SAC), where they can consult with a wide range of representatives of user groups, preparers, financial analysts, academics, auditors, regulators, and professional accounting bodies that are affected by, and interested in, the IASB's work. Similar to the FASAC, the SAC provides input on the development and potential impact of standards.

The 14 current IASB members (12 full-time and two part-time) were selected to form a broad geographical and professional representation. They include former Big Four partners, academics, and country-level standard setters from China, Japan, France, the UK, and the US. The IASB's principle responsibilities are to develop and issue IFRS and to approve interpretations developed by the International Financial Reporting Interpretations Committee (IFRIC). The IFRIC develops interpretations of specific standards with a goal of reaching consensus on the appropriate accounting treatment and to provide authoritative guidance on those issues. When forming those interpretations, IFRIC works closely with national committees and considers both newly identified financial reporting issues that have not been dealt with in IFRS and issues where there is no authoritative guidance and unsatisfactory or conflicting interpretations have or may develop.

One important difference between the FASB and the IASB is the way in which each board is funded. In 2002 the US Congress passed the Sarbanes-Oxley Act (SOX). This bill established the Public Company Accounting Oversight Board (PCAOB), which regulates accounting firms in their role as auditors, and specific funding for the FASB and its activities through a fee assessed on publicly traded firms. A critical reason for Congress's decision to assess this fee was to increase the independence of the FASB in the face of several significant US accounting scandals. In contrast, the IASB is funded through donations, ultimately providing a less certain stream of funds than the mandated funding through SOX. A number of groups and individuals, including the SEC, have expressed significant concerns with how the IASB is funded and its potential impact on the independence of the IASB.

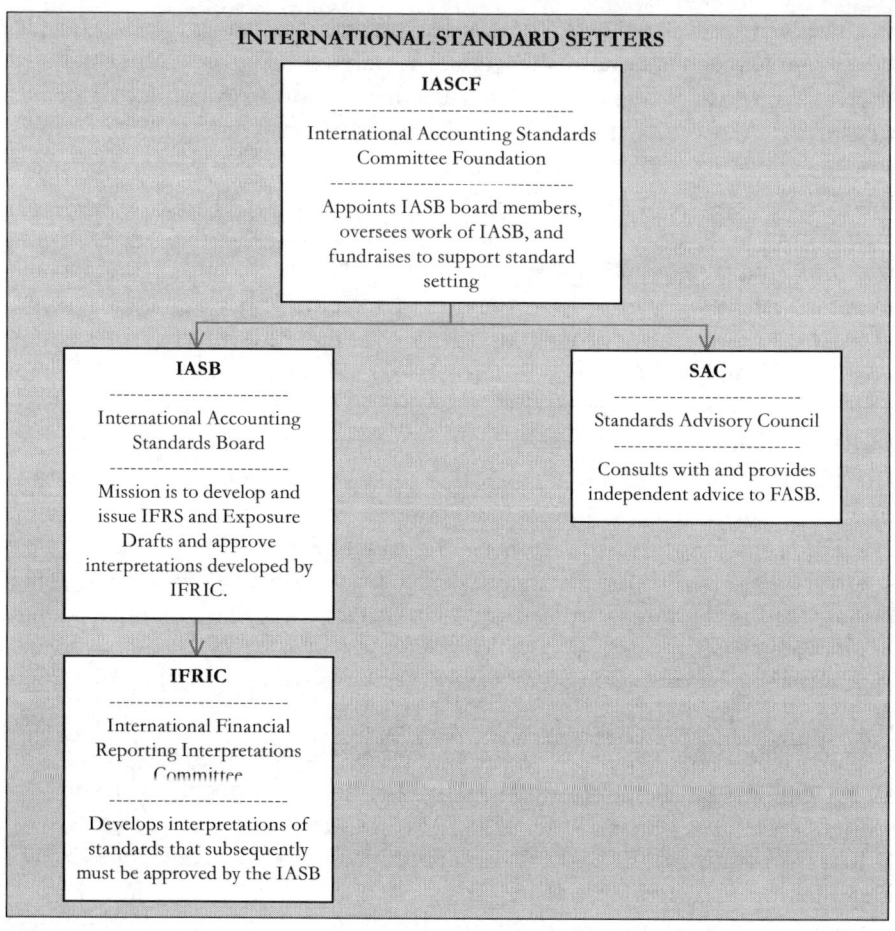

Security Markt Regulators

There is a strong role for regulation of the security markets in the ability of any set of accounting standards to consistently capture economic activity across time and companies. Without regulation, firms may inconsistently apply standards or apply standards inappropriately, reducing the quality and/or comparability of resulting financial reports. Thus, it is important to remember that security market regulators wield significant influence throughout the world and, ultimately, are key players in the ability of a single set of accounting standards to effectively provide comparable financial reports across jurisdictions. Regulation of the world's security markets and the information produced for stakeholders in those markets is particularly important as stocks, bonds, and other securities can lose value, unlike banking deposits that may be guaranteed by some governments.

A key element of security market regulation that differs from accounting standard setting is its lack of centralization. Unlike accounting standard setting, security market regulation is dispersed across numerous regulators. Typically, each security market is regulated by its own regulator (e.g., the Dutch Stock Exchange is regulated by the Autoriteit Financiele Markten, the UK Stock Exchange is regulated by the Financial Services Authority, and the US stock markets are regulated by the SEC). This lack of centralization in the regulation of the security markets is a significant, potential impediment to any set of standards producing consistent financial reports. Financial reports produced by firms are filed with and regulated by the security markets where those firms are traded. Even if a single set of accounting standards is available and adopted across jurisdictions, without consistent regulation of the filings based on those standards, significant variation in the application of those accounting standards could arise and result in inconsistent financial reports. Virtually all security markets have their own regulators who control the application of accounting standards within their jurisdiction. Security market regulators understand this concern and have begun to work together to establish means to improve the consistent regulation of accounting standard setters across various security markets. Our discussion centers on some of the most influential security regulators and regulator groups in the move toward the adoption of IFRS throughout the world. US security market regulators (the SEC), influential organizations (the European Securities Commission (ESC) and the Committee of European Security Regulators (CESR)), and two security regulator groups (the International Organization of Securities Commissions (IOSCO) and the International Accounting Standards Committee Monitoring Groups (IASCF Monitoring Group)) are currently active at an international level and are considered crucial in the regulation of US GAAP and/or IFRS.

US Security Market Regulator
One of the more mature security regulators in the world is the US security regulator, the Securities and Exchange Commission (SEC), which was formed through the Securities Exchange Act of 1934. The SEC is a federally funded agency, granted statutory authority to establish financial accounting and reporting standards for publicly held companies. Throughout its history the Commission's policy has been to rely on the private sector (e.g., the FASB) for this function. Decisions made by the SEC to achieve its stated mission 'to protect investors, maintain fair, orderly, and efficient markets, and facilitate capital formation' have had a strong influence on the growing acceptance of IFRS throughout the world. Many have suggested that the adoption of a single, high-quality, and comprehensive set of accounting standards will produce transparent financial reports and, thereby, lower the cost of capital and facilitate capital formation. Given that link between capital formation and the adoption of a single set of accounting standards and the benefit of this that accrues to US investors, the SEC has been a strong advocate of improving the quality of IFRS and the convergence between US GAAP and IFRS.

Though it is the primary overseer and regulator of the US securities markets, the SEC works closely with many other institutions, including Congress, federal departments and agencies, self-regulatory organizations (e.g., the stock exchanges), state securities regulators, and various private sector organizations. The US president appoints five individuals to head the SEC, four Commissioners and one Chairman—the SEC Commissioners. One division and one office of the SEC are particularly involved in setting accounting standards—the Division of Corporate Finance (DCF) and the Office of the Chief Accountant (OCA). The DCF is required to review firm financial reports filed with the SEC (including annual and quarterly filings (forms 10-K and 10-Q)) to determine whether the information provided meets the appropriate accounting standards under US GAAP. If, in the DCF staff's assessment, a firm falls short in its requirement to do so, the DCF contacts the firm and requests the additional information or requests changes to the information provided. Firms are allowed to respond to DCF staff comments and, if necessary, to make changes to its reports to comply with US GAAP. Through its evaluations of filed financial statements, the DCF often becomes aware of areas where multiple firms fail to report fully or correctly report or to disclose information required by US GAAP. The DCF shares this information with the OCA and the FASB to assist the regulators and standard setters as they consider areas where accounting standards may be inadequate or poorly understood.

European Union Security Market Regulators

Two security market regulators established by the European Union (EU) are the European Securities Committee (ESC) and the Committee of European Security Regulators (CESR). The EU, a political and economic union of twenty-seven 'member states' located (primarily) in Europe, was established in 1993. One of its primary objectives was to develop a common market across its member states by reducing barriers to trade with a long-term goal of enhancing growth throughout the area. The EU, which utilizes the euro as its primary form of currency, generated an estimated gross domestic product of almost $17 trillion (almost 31% of world-wide output) making it the largest economy in the world. Its 2002 decision to require all EU listed firms to adopt IFRS by 2005 was critical in the international acceptance of IFRS. The European Commission serves as the executive branch of the EU, responsible for proposing legislation and upholding treaties. The ESC and CESR were formed in 2001 by the European Commission on the recommendation of 'The Committee of Wise Men on the Regulation of Securities Market' (its real name!) to assist the European Commission in regulatory issues.

The ESC is composed of high-level representatives from the EU member states. The European Commission consults the ESC when drafting legislative proposals related to securities issues for advice on policy issues in the securities field. The ESC also develops basic legislation and promotes consistent implementation measures between national regulators. The CESR is composed of high-level representatives of the national public authorities who are considered knowledgeable in securities issues. The CESR operates more independently than the ESC although it also advises the European Commission on policy issues related to securities issues. Ultimately, both the ESC and the CESR advise the European Commission on similar issues, but play different roles. As the European Commission drafts legislative proposals it may consult both the ESC and the CESR; when preparing the draft measures, the European Commission often consults with the ESC and then assigns preparation of the technical details to the CESR. Some have suggested that the ESC and the CESR are simply a precursor to a "European SEC"—an independent administrative agency responsible for regulating securities issues for the European Union.

International Organization of Securities Commissions
In 1984 securities regulators from North and South America joined with regulators from France, Indonesia, Korea, and the UK to form the International Organization of Securities Commissions (IOSCO) as an outgrowth of its predecessor regional association. IOSCO provides comprehensive technical assistance to its members and seeks member cooperation to improve domestic and international financial markets, establish standards, and ensure the integrity of markets by rigorous application of standards and enforcement. In 1998, IOSCO adopted disclosure standards that allowed multinational companies to prepare a single nonfinancial statement disclosure document for cross-border securities offerings and stock exchange listings. In 1999 the SEC adopted these IOSCO disclosure standards. In 2005 IOSCO adopted a multilateral memorandum of understanding (IOSCO MOU) designed to facilitate cross-border enforcement and exchange of information among the international community of securities regulators.

Currently, IOSCO members regulate more than one hundred jurisdictions that encompass more than 90% of the world securities markets (including those in China, Germany, India, Japan, the UK, and the US). Its role is to increase cooperation among security regulators to promote high standards of regulation, to exchange information in order to promote the development of domestic markets, to unite to establish regulatory standards, and to promote the integrity of the markets through consistent application of the standards and effective enforcement. While IOSCO members are influential in the adoption of IFRS, ultimately it is the members, not IOSCO, that are responsible for regulation.

IASCF Monitoring Group
Another group that has influenced the adoption of IFRS is the IASCF Monitoring Group. This group provides a formal link between the IASB and securities market regulators around the world; the initial membership includes a

member from the European Commission, the managing director of the International Monetary Fund, the chair of the IOSCO Emerging Markets Committee, the chair of the IOSCO Technical Committee, the commissioner of the Japan Financial Services Agency, the chairman of the SEC, and the president of the World Bank. In June 2008 representatives of the IOSCO, the SEC, the European Commission, and the Japan Financial Services Agency participated in discussions organized by the IASCF, with the goal of creating the IASCF Monitoring Group. In the US, the SEC and the FASB have a long-standing working relationship on US GAAP; the proposed convergence of US GAAP and IFRS has left securities regulators around the world with questions about possible interactions/conflicts with the IASB. The IASCF Monitoring Group is an autonomous group, comprised of 'public authorities generally charged with the adoption or recognition of financial reporting standards and international organizations with a mandate that includes facilitating the development and effective functioning of capital markets.' In a joint statement at the June 2008 meeting, the various regulators stated, "The increased adoption and use of IFRS in capital markets around the world necessitates strengthening the accountability of the foundation to the authorities responsible for setting financial disclosure requirements by public companies." The IASCF Monitoring Group's role will be designed to ensure the independence of the IASB, while reinforcing the public interest oversight provided by the IASCF trustees.

While our discussion of security market regulators is limited, we want to emphasize the importance of established stock exchanges and their regulators that continue to have an impact on the development and adoption of IFRS. For example, the Financial Services Authority (FSA) regulates the London Stock Exchange and its associated market, the Alternative Investment Market. As of 2005 the FSA required all listed firms to apply IFRS; additionally, those firms must comply with the Combined Code of Corporate Governance issued by the UK Financial Reporting Council.

The issue of security market regulation and whether regulators will consistently apply accounting standards across jurisdictions continues to be a concern in attaining benefits from the adoption of a single set of accounting standards. Critics suggest that, without a single cohesive group of securities regulators to provide consistent regulation of IFRS, the hoped for increase in comparability and positive effects of moving to a single set of standards will not be realized. Furthermore, without consistent enforcement, there is concern that the quality of the financial reports produced will be of sufficiently high quality.

Auditors and Audit Regulators

Auditors play a key role in the application of accounting standards across firms and jurisdictions. An auditor is an independent certified public accountant who examines the financial statements prepared by a company's management and provides a written report that includes an opinion as to whether the financial statements and related disclosures are 'fairly stated' and 'comply in all material respects with GAAP.' The GAAP required is a function of where the firm files its financial reports and the rules established by the security market regulator. For example, US firms that file with the SEC are required to provide audited annual reports prepared using US GAAP, while EU firms are required to provide audited annual reports prepared using IFRS.

There are two facts to keep in mind as we discuss international regulation of audits and auditors. First, management, not the auditor, is charged with preparing its firm's financial reports. This means that the day-to-day recording of transactions, the selection of what GAAP to use, the application of accounting standards, and decisions including estimates and judgments regarding specific issues, are all the responsibility of management. The auditor provides the public with additional assurance, beyond managements' statements, that information contained in the statements is free of material errors and based on a specific set of accounting standards (e.g., US GAAP or IFRS). Second, auditors provide no guarantees that the numbers reported are correct nor do they certify that fraud or all errors are absent. In short, auditors attest to whether the financial information presented by management is 'fairly stated' (free of misleading material and/or important and significant errors) and that the statements have been prepared in accordance with the set of accounting standards selected by management. It is important to note that auditor reports on financial statements are neither evaluations nor opinions as to the financial health, performance, attractiveness, potential, or any other similar determination of the firm in question.

As a group of professionals whose professional responsibility is to ensure that a specific set of standards is appropriately applied across various firms, auditors are well versed in issues that arise in the application of those standards. Thus, they are key players in the evolution of international accounting standards. Auditors and auditing itself is regulated. Since auditors serve as gatekeepers, variation in the regulation of that group can have a significant effect on how standards are applied across various jurisdictions. Regulation of auditors is often linked with security market regulation, as *audited* financial reports typically are required to be filed by firms in order for the firm to trade within a given security market. As with security regulation, audit regulation is provided by a variety of groups internationally. Our focus will be on those that have a more significant international impact.

Public Company Accounting Oversight Board
Currently, the Public Company Accounting Oversight Board [PCAOB] regulates auditors in their role as they audit publicly traded corporations in the US. The PCAOB is a private, nonprofit corporation established by the Sarbanes-Oxley Act of 2002 to protect investors and the public interest by promoting informative,

fair, and independent audit reports. The PCAOB consists of five full-time members appointed by the SEC, including two CPAs. It has the power to set standards for auditing, quality control, ethics, and independence related to the preparation of audit reports; conduct inspections of registered public accounting firms; and impose appropriate sanctions to improve the quality of audit services. Currently, the PCAOB has adopted a formal set of auditing standards (Generally Accepted Auditing Standards or GAAS) that lay out the principles to which an auditor must adhere to perform an audit.

International Auditing and Assurance Standards Board
The International Auditing and Assurance Standards Board (IAASB), established in 1978 as the International Auditing Practices Committee, sets standards that deal with auditing and other assurance services in an international context. It has published 32 International Standards on Auditing (ISA), analogous to GAAS established within the US, and is instrumental in facilitating the convergence of national and international auditing standards. Over 100 countries use or are in the process of adopting or incorporating the ISA issued by the IAASB into their national auditing standards or using them as a basis for preparing national auditing standards. The board has grown from 11 members to 18 members; more than 112 professionals from 28 countries, including Canada, China, France, Germany, Japan, the UK, and the US, have participated as IAPC/IAASB members.

International Forum of Independent Audit Regulators
The International Forum of Independent Audit Regulators (IFIAR), established in 2006, was formed to share knowledge of the audit market environment and practical experience of independent audit regulatory activity and to promote collaboration and consistency in regulatory activity. Its members include the Australian Securities and Investments Commission, the Canadian Public Accountability Board, the Certified Public Accountants and Auditing Oversight Board (Japan), the UK Financial Reporting Council, and the PCAOB. While audit regulation within countries is common, international regulation of auditors and the auditing profession is still developing. Similar to security market regulation, international regulation of audits and the audit profession is an integral component of the adoption of IFRS throughout the world.

Pause and Reflect: *There are three groups of interested parties that directly affect both the widespread adoption of IFRS throughout the world and the eventual ability of that adoption to improve financial reporting. Name those three groups (in general), specific entities within those groups, and the roles that they play in the adoption of accounting standards. Prepare an 'organizational chart' that maps how these groups interact, considering their relative influence and regulatory authority. In your analysis, make use of more detailed and current information about these groups available via the Internet and other sources.*

SETTING ACCOUNTING STANDARDS

US GAAP

Prior to the passage of the 1933 and 1934 securities acts, no group formally issued accounting standards in the US. Since that time, the SEC has chosen to rely on the private sector to develop and enforce accounting standards. In 1973 the SEC formally established that the set of standards drafted by the FASB and its predecessor organizations are considered US Generally Accepted Accounting Principles (US GAAP). As stated earlier, US firms that file with the SEC are required to use US GAAP in those filings. Non-US firms required to file with the SEC (foreign firms who elect to list on the US security markets, called 'Foreign Private Issuers' (FPI)) are not required to apply US GAAP in their statements. However, until 2007, as a footnote in their filed statements, FPIs were required to disclose the set of standards they applied and to provide a reconciliation from the earnings and stockholders' equity based on the GAAP employed within their financial reports to US GAAP.

The SEC retains broad statutory powers to define accounting terms, prescribe methods to be followed in preparing financial reports, and specify the details to be presented in the financial statements. Nonetheless, the SEC continues to rely on the private sector and the accounting profession to set accounting standards. As of September 2008 US GAAP established by the FASB and its predecessor boards included a total of 163 standards, several of which have been superseded or modified after adoption. In addition to the standards themselves, the FASB (through the former Standards Interpretations Committee (SIC)) issues interpretations of the standards. These interpretations, which typically modify or extend the standards, are also considered US GAAP. Technical bulletins, another type of pronouncement issued by the FASB, are designed to provide specific and timely guidance when dealing with particular financial reporting problems.

IFRS

Prior to 1973 a single set of international accounting standards did not exist, as each country set their own set of standards. However, as capital markets increased and cross-border barriers decreased, many groups and countries began to call for a single set of high-quality, comprehensive accounting standards for all countries and firms to use. As early as 1966 accountants within the Canada, the UK, and the US created the Accountants International Study Group as a means to enhance the development of comparable standards and, ultimately, the harmonization of accounting standards. In 1972, at the 10th World Congress of Accountants, a UK representative proposed the establishment of an international group to establish a single set of standards for all countries to use. The International Accounting Standards Committee, the precursor to the IASB, was formed in 1973, with voting representatives from nine countries: Australia, Canada, France, Germany, Japan, the Netherlands, Mexico, the US, and the UK. This board was empowered to establish International Accounting Standards (IAS).

In the early 1990's there was a push to improve the overall quality and international applicability of the IAS. In 1994, the IOSCO completed a review of the then-current IAS and recommended areas that they believed required improvement before they were willing to endorse the cross-border use of IAS. At the same time, the IASC Advisory Council was approved to provide oversight to the IASC and manage its finances. In 1995 the IOSCO and the IASC agreed a "Core Standards Work Program" in response to the 1994 review. The European Commission supported this agreement and began to 'associate itself' with the IASC's work, lending additional credibility to the IAS. The Standing Interpretations Committee was established in 1997 to provide interpretations of the standards. By 2000 the IASC had expanded to include all the members of the International Federation of Accountants (IFAC), including 152 professional accounting bodies in 112 countries. In addition to the official board members, a number of organizations act as official observers, including the FASB, the European Commission, the Ministry of Finance of the People's Republic of China, and IOSCO. Forty-one International Accounting Standards (IASs) were developed by the IASC prior to its reorganization and the establishment of the International Accounting Standards Board (IASB) in 2001. Currently, IFRS include the 29 of the 41 IAS that were adopted and not superseded by the IASC and the 8 IFRS developed and adopted by the IASB. Similar to US GAAP, IFRS refers to the entire body of IASB pronouncements, including standards and interpretations approved by the IASB and IFRIC as well as their predecessors, IASC and SIC.

IFRS Use Internationally

IAS, the precursor to IFRS, have been available for adoption since the 1990s. However, their widespread use and adoption was limited until early in the 2000s. Several events have had significant impacts on the development and increasing use of IFRS and, ultimately, on the potential adoption of IFRS in the US. In 2002 two events took place that significantly affected the widespread adoption of IFRS. First, the EC's decision to adopt IAS (IFRS) from 2005 onwards was an important milestone in the widespread acceptance of IFRS and is considered by many to be a primary driver behind its expanded use. Also in 2002, the Norwalk Agreement, an agreement between the FASB and IASB leading toward eventual convergence between US GAAP and IAS/IFRS, was executed. This agreement constituted another significant step in the acceptance of IFRS as high-quality, comprehensive accounting standards, which affected the willingness of companies and countries to adopt IFRS.

An additional event that has affected international acceptance of IFRS was the SEC's decision to eliminate the reconciliation requirement in the annual filings for FPIs that adopted IFRS. This decision, proposed in July 2007, was adopted in December 2007 and effective for filings for financial years ending after November 15, 2007. In making the rule change, the SEC reduced filing costs for FPIs that employed IFRS to encourage more companies to list on the US markets. In addition, many have suggested that the SEC's acceptance of IFRS on par with US GAAP is consistent with the Commission believing that the two sets of accounting standards provide financial reports of equal quality.

IFRS Use in the US

In November 2008 the SEC issued a proposing release that detailed a 'roadmap' of specific items that it believed must be addressed prior to the use of IFRS by US companies filing in the US and asked for public comments on its proposal. In its proposal, the SEC stated that, if approved, it would allow approximately 110 of the largest publicly held companies in the US (approximately 14% of the US market capitalization), those that are among the top 20 in their industries according to market capitalization, to begin using IFRS by as early as 2010 filings (fiscal periods ending after December 15, 2009). In addition, the proposing release suggested that US companies would be required to transition to IFRS (in lieu of US GAAP) as early as 2014. The SEC roadmap included four specific milestones it will consider before deciding whether to adopt IFRS for all US firms. The milestones are (1) improvements in accounting standards; (2) increased accountability of the IASCF in terms of funding that ensures independence; (3) an assessment of the IFRS transition process by early adopters, including the cost and acceptance by stakeholders; and (4) education and training in the US relating to IFRS.

Why IFRS?

While it is becoming increasingly evident that IFRS has become widely accepted internationally, why is there interest in the adoption of IFRS in the US? While many believe the adoption of IFRS in the US is inevitable, including the AICPA, the SEC chairman Christopher Cox, and the Big Four accounting firms, not everyone agrees this is in the best interest of US investors. On one hand, advocates for the adoption of IFRS in the US suggest that, in today's global economy, a single set of accounting standards will benefit all participants in the capital markets and company stakeholders by streamlining costs for firms that operate globally and increasing comparability of financial statements. Public companies that operate in multiple jurisdictions will benefit in the ability to use a single set of accounting standards across subsidiaries and groups domiciled across multiple jurisdictions. Investors will be better able to compare financial results and the financial positions of reporting firms around the world, allowing them to make better investment decisions without artificial barriers to translate. Companies will be able to present their information in a way comparable to their competitors, again reducing artificial barriers to such comparisons. A single set of accounting standards will benefit preparers, investors, bankers, and creditors, as it will simplify the learning process by allowing a focus on a single set of accounting standards, rather than multiple sets. However, the benefits that might accrue are contingent on the adoption of a set of high-quality, comprehensive standards.

Many are concerned that IFRS is not as 'robust' as US GAAP, thus the financial reports prepared using IFRS will be less transparent and perhaps even reduce comparability, that the cost of transition will be high, and that the US market is not prepared for the transition. Based on the transition to IFRS in Europe, experts estimate that implementation will take companies two to three years. Changing from US GAAP to IFRS will require firms to gather the necessary information, make modifications to accounting and control systems, and perhaps even renegotiate debt and other agreements currently linked to financial performance measured using US GAAP. In addition, there is significant concern that there will be a lack of professionals familiar with IFRS. Knowledge of IFRS will be a valuable asset as you enter the workplace during this time of dynamic change in the accounting environment.

In addition, if (when?) the decision is made to employ IFRS in the US, there are additional factors to consider. Ultimately, in order for US investors to benefit from the adoption of IFRS in the US, the adoption of that set of standards must also include changes to security regulation and the auditing regulatory environment. Without commensurate changes to the security regulation and for auditors and the audit process, the adoption of a single set of accounting standards is less likely to bring about net positive impacts.

Pause and Reflect: *The adoption of IFRS throughout the world has changed rapidly across time. Using the information above and more current information drawn from the Internet and other sources, draw a timeline of the process of adoption of IFRS around the world, highlighting significant events in that process (e.g., the decision by the EU to require the use of IFRS). Consider where the US is in the process of considering the adoption of IFRS, based on comment letters (available via the SEC website) and other sources that reflect the opinions and perspectives of various constituencies. Has the credit crises and the recession impacted this decision? Consider comments made by Mary Schapiro (the chairman of the SEC) and others regarding this issue in your discussion.*

Resources:
Financial Accounting Foundation – FAF –
http://www.fasb.org/faf/index2.shtml.
International Accounting Standards Committee Foundation – IASCF
http://www.iasplus.com/restruct/iascf.htm
Emerging Issues Tax Force - EITF –
http://www.fasb.org/eitf/eiftissu.shtml
Financial Accounting Standards Advisory Committee – FASAC –
http://www.fasb.org/fasac/
SEC proposing release –
http://www.sec.gov/news/press/2008/2008-184.htm
International Forum of Independent Audit Regulators – IFIAR –
http://www.ifiar.org/
International Accounting Standards Committee Foundation – IASCF –
http://www.iasplus.com/restruct/iascf.htm
International Auditing and Assurance Standards Board – IAASB –
http://www.ifac.org/iaasb/
IASCF Monitoring Group –
http://www.sec.gov/news/press/2008/2008-112.htm
International Organization of Securities Commissions – IOSCO –
http://www.iosco.org/
European Securities Commission – ESC –
http://ec.europa.eu/internal_market/securities/esc/index_en.htm
International Organization of Securities Commissions – CESR –
http://www.cesr-eu.org/index.php?page=home&mac=0&id=
Office of Chief Accountant – OCA of the SEC –
http://www.sec.gov/about/offices/oca.htm
Division of Corporate Finance – DCF of the SEC –
http://www.sec.gov/divisions/corpfin.shtml
SEC Commissioners – http://www.sec.gov/about/commissioner.shtml
Securities and Exchange Commission – SEC – http://www.sec.gov/
International Financial Reporting Interpretations Committee – IFRIC –
http://www.iasplus.com/interps/interps.htm
Standards Advisory Committee – SAC –
http://www.iasb.org/about+us/about+the+SAC/about+the+SAC.htm

CHAPTER 3
CONCEPTUAL FRAMEWORK

In this chapter we provide a discussion of conceptual frameworks and how differences in them and in the application of standards based on them cause differences in financial reports. This section begins our discussion of not simply where there are differences between US GAAP and IFRS financial reports but *why* those differences arise. As part of this discussion, we will refer to relevant items in the Exposure Draft on establishing an improved common conceptual framework, jointly published by the FASB/IASB.

Before beginning our discussion, we consider an important underlying assumption that underlies all accounting standards—perspective. Accounting standard setters and standard setting itself either implicitly or explicitly presumes an audience for the financial reports provided. While both the FASB and IASB view financial report users as decision makers, many suggest that the primary audience for these reports are investors and that, in general, financial reports that meet investors' information needs will also meet most of the needs of other stakeholders. This belief is predicated on stakeholders having a common interest in the ability of an enterprise to generate cash and cash equivalents and in the timing and certainty of those cash flows. However, inherent conflicts exist among different stakeholders' information needs. Selecting the information needs of one stakeholder group over another may influence the recording of a particular transaction or group of transactions. Realistically, it is difficult (if not impossible) for a single set of accounting standards that provide financial reports to meet the information needs of all stakeholder groups simultaneously. This inability to meet the information needs of all means that the perspective adopted by standard setters matters. In fact, in making specific decisions, it is sometimes deemed necessary to trade off the needs of one group against the needs of another, affecting the development and application of standards themselves. If the perspective of the standard setters is that of investors, their needs will dominate. However, if the perspective of the standard setters is that of a broader community, such as the geographical area within which the firm operates, a different standard may obtain. Consequently, perspective may be an important component of understanding standard setters' decisions and the final standards that are adopted.

WHAT IS A CONCEPTUAL FRAMEWORK

Accounting standards provide the structure through which managers and preparers make decisions regarding the appropriate accounting for transactions. Similarly, a conceptual framework provides the structure through which standard setters make decisions in setting accounting standards. A conceptual framework is a body of interrelated objectives (which identify the goals and purposes of financial reporting) and fundamentals (the underlying concepts that help achieve those objectives) that underlie the standard-setting process. These concepts are integral to the standard-setting process and have far-reaching effects. They provide guidance to standard setters as they consider the transactions, events, and circumstances to be accounted for, determine how those selected items should be recognized and measured, and, subsequently, how the recognized and measured items should be summarized and reported.

Both the FASB and the IASB employ conceptual frameworks in the standard-setting process that are more similar than different. Because of the link between the conceptual frameworks and accounting standards, understanding differences between the FASB and IASB conceptual frameworks is instrumental in understanding sources of differences in accounting standards promulgated by them. In this spirit, we briefly discuss the current FASB and IASB conceptual frameworks focusing on differences between them. In addition, we discuss the joint FASB/IASB project to establish a single conceptual framework and where the boards appear to be heading, as evidenced by their joint exposure draft.

Several general assumptions underlie the preparation and presentation of financial reports, specifically stated in the FASB's and IASB's discussions of their conceptual frameworks. The FASB highlights four assumptions: (1) economic firm; (2) going concern; (3) monetary unit; and (4) periodicity; the IASB highlights two assumptions: (1) accrual basis accounting; and (2) going concern. While each board highlights different underlying assumptions, both boards start from practically the same point in terms of explicit and implicit assumptions underlying the preparation of financial statements.

Conceptual Framework

The conceptual frameworks can be sorted into three levels. The first defines the objectives of financial reporting; the second explains the qualitative characteristics of accounting information and defines the elements of financial statements; the third level explains 'which, when, and how' the financial elements and events should be recognized, measured, and reported.

Objectives

The objectives of financial reporting in the US GAAP and IFRS frameworks are similar in tone in that they both state that the purpose of financial statements is to 'provide information' that 'is useful' to stakeholders. Differences arise in the focus, in terms of stakeholders, of the respective frameworks. The US GAAP framework centers on capital providers—investors, creditors and other users in making rational investment, credit, and similar decisions. While the IFRS framework includes these users, it also specifically lists employees, customers, governments and their agencies, and the public as users. These broader user groups may be reflected in differing perspectives in the standard-setting process. The joint exposure draft reinforces the importance of 'present and potential capital providers' with the belief that 'Information that is decision useful to capital providers may also be useful to other users of financial reporting who are not capital providers.' The proposed objective calls for financial information to be prepared from the perspective of the entity, explicitly elevating the need to inform capital providers. This new objective could be interpreted as subjugating stewardship-relevant information in favor of valuation-relevant information.

Level 2
Qualitative Characteristics of Information

The FASB framework considers two 'primary decision-specific qualities' of information, (relevance and reliability) and two secondary qualitative characteristics of information (comparability and consistency). In a similar manner, the IASB framework identifies what it considers four principal qualitative characteristics: relevance, reliability, comparability, and understandability. Both boards acknowledge the importance of timeliness and materiality in providing relevant information. Three of the four characteristics of what each board considers essential qualities of useful information are the same, although there are some differences in the definitions. The differences between the boards' views on providing useful information seem to be the importance of consistency to the FASB (the consistent use of accounting methods) versus the IASB's focus on understandability (information being presented in a manner that users with 'a reasonable knowledge of business and economic activities and accounting and who are willing to study it diligently' will be able to readily understand). However, a careful reading of the frameworks suggests that these differences are less consequential than they appear. For example, while the FASB framework does not explicitly discuss the issue of understandability in its objective of financial reporting, there is an explicit statement alluding to the issue of understandability. In general, the FASB and IASB frameworks consider the same qualitative characteristics.

The joint Exposure Draft asserts two fundamental qualitative characteristics of decision useful information—relevance and faithful representation. The second characteristic suggests a renewed focus on the importance of information 'faithfully representing' the economic phenomenon it is purported to represent, which may be seen as a shift towards substance over form. It may also be that the boards have chosen not to use the term 'reliable,' which suggests a level of certainty that may not be obtainable. (In prior frameworks, faithful representation was considered a component of reliable information.) The joint draft goes on to emphasize the importance of providing information that is complete, neutral, and free from material error for it to 'faithfully represent' the economics. In addition, the draft considers four 'enhancing qualitative characteristics': comparability, verifiability, timeliness, and understandability.

level 3

Elements of Financial Statements

Both boards' conceptual frameworks include explicit guidance on the required elements, or building blocks, of financial statements, including assets, liabilities, equity, revenues, and expenses. The FASB includes three additional items: gains, losses, and comprehensive income. While the IASB framework does not specifically address these three items, its definitions of income (expenses) encompass the FASB's of gains and losses. Likewise, the FASB's definition of comprehensive income is very similar to the IASB's concept of 'capital and capital maintenance.' Even so, as we consider differences between the two sets of standards, it is important to understand that there will be times where apparently synonymous items (e.g., income and revenues) are subtlety different, while apparently unrelated items (e.g., comprehensive income and capital maintenance) are very similar in concept. Even minor differences in defining critical terms (like an asset) across the conceptual frameworks can cause differences in the sets of standards that arise from those frameworks and, ultimately, differences in how particular transactions are recorded.

The joint FASB/IASB conceptual framework project on defining the elements of the financial statements is still in its early stages. At this point, the boards have agreed that the current frameworks' existing asset definitions have a series of shortcomings and have tentatively adopted the 'working' definition as follows: "An *asset* of a firm is a present economic resource to which the firm has a right or other access that others do not have." They include 'amplifying text' which serves to define specific terms in the definition (like 'present' and 'economic resource'). It is essential for the boards to carefully and concisely define concepts within the new conceptual framework in order for it to provide structure in the standard-setting process as very minor differences in wording can have substantial impacts. The definition of an asset is particularly crucial, as many of the other elements are defined with reference to assets. While the final definition is not determined, it is interesting to note that the current working definition focuses on current value, without reference to 'future economic benefit' or 'past transaction or event' included in the FASB/IASB current definitions of assets.

ELEMENTS OF FINANCIAL STATEMENTS
Asset – A probable future economic benefit obtained or controlled by an entity as a result of a past transaction or event.
Comprehensive Income – The change in equity of an entity during a period from transactions and other events and circumstances from non-owner sources.
Earnings/Income – Increases in economic benefits during the accounting period in the form on inflows or enhancements of assets or decreases of liabilities that result in increases in equity, other than those relating to contributions from equity participants. A measure of entity performance during
Equity/Net Assets – The ownership interest in the assets of an entity that remains after paying its liabilities.
Expenses – Outflows or use of assets or incurrence of liabilities from delivering or producing goods, rendering services, or carrying out other activities that constitute the entity's ongoing or major or central operations.
Gains – Similar to revenues except they result from peripheral or incidental transactions of an entity.
Liabilities – Probable future sacrifices of economics benefits arising from present obligations of a particular entity to transfer assets or provide services to other entities in the future as a result of past transactions or events.
Losses – Similar to expenses except they result from peripheral or incidental transactions of an entity.
Revenues – Inflows or other enhancements of assets of an entity or settlements of its liabilities from delivering or producing goods, rendering services, or other activities that constitute the entity's ongoing major or central operations.

Recognition, Measurement, and Reporting
The boards' conceptual frameworks tend to define three aspects of accounting—recognition, measurement, and reporting—in relatively similar manners. Recognition is the 'process of incorporating in the balance sheet or income statement an item that meets the definition of an element.' While both boards define the term similarly, they do acknowledge differences in some specific criteria to meet that definition and note that neither current framework addresses issues related to derecognizing items. Financial statement elements are recognized when it is both 'probable that any future economic benefit associated with the item will flow to or from the enterprise' and 'the item's cost or value can be measured with reliability.' However, differences between when US GAAP and IFRS determine specific transactions meet the standard for recognition are a significant driver in differences in financial reports prepared

under US GAAP and IFRS. Another area related to recognition in which there are significant differences between US GAAP and IFRS is in the area of revenue recognition and in determining when and how specific types of revenue should be recognized. This is an area where the issue of 'principles versus rules' truly exists. US GAAP has revenue recognition guidance that encompasses more than a hundred standards, while IFRS has two main revenue recognition standards that are 'inconsistent and vague' (as described by the IASB). In their joint project, the boards are actively working to resolve and eliminate differences in the specifics related to recognition and provide a basis for resolving the issue of derecognition.

Measurement, required in order to recognize an item, assigns monetary amounts to the elements. This critical aspect of financial reporting is quite underdeveloped in the current conceptual frameworks. Both frameworks provide lists of measurement bases, but neither provides guidance in choosing among them or considering other alternatives. Thus, measurement is an area where there can be significant differences across US GAAP and IFRS in the adoption and application of standards. It is also an area where much work remains to be done to establish a single framework. As of this point, the boards' progress on this issue within the joint conceptual framework project has been to establish a list of measurement basis candidates and how they might be defined.

Currently, both boards state that a complete set of financial statements includes an income statement, statement of financial position, statement of cash flows, and statement of shareholders' equity and disclosures through footnotes. If you lay two sets of financial statements side by side, one based on US GAAP and the other based on IFRS, you will find that they may look different, but tend to report very similar information. At least some of the differences can be characterized as cosmetic—the statements may look different but report the same information. Many of the other differences that arise are due to fundamental issues related to recognition and measurement between either the standards themselves or the application of the standards. We will discuss these in greater detail in later sections. However, the joint financial statement presentation project includes a number of significant changes to how information will be reported.

CONCLUSION

While the FASB and the IASB conceptual frameworks are quite similar, subtle differences between them may cause differences in financial reports produced by the application of US GAAP versus IFRS. In short, while the two frameworks share many fundamental principles, there are times when they are implemented and applied in different manners. In addition, there are areas within the conceptual frameworks that are underdeveloped (i.e., measurement) or missing (i.e., derecognition) where significant differences in accounting can be found. Finally, there are areas in the frameworks where concepts are defined similarly, but differences in accounting arise due to differences in the interpretation of terms and concepts based on cultural differences that exist across countries.

Resources:
FASB/IASB joint Exposure Draft: Conceptual Framework Project
http://www.fasb.org/project/conceptual_framework.shtml
FASB/ISB joint Financial Statement Presentation Project
http://www.fasb.org/project/financial_statement_presentation.shtml

CHAPTER 4:
US GAAP AND IFRS—AN EXAMPLE

In this chapter we describe a pair of publicly available 2006 annual reports from two firms in the 'agricultural chemicals' industry, Monsanto and Syngenta. Monsanto applies US GAAP and Syngenta applies IFRS to prepare their financial reports. The annual reports are available via the Web links at the end of the chapter. We use annual reports from 2006 as it allows us to include a company-prepared reconciliation that details specific differences between what Syngenta reports after applying IFRS and what it would have reported if it had applied US GAAP. The IFRS net income/stockholders' equity to US GAAP net income/stockholders' equity reconciliations along with detailed explanations of the source of those differences was prepared by Syngenta to fulfill an SEC requirement in order for it to trade on US stock markets. The purpose of referencing these annual reports and this discussion is to increase your familiarity (and comfort level) with differences across financial reports prepared using US GAAP versus those prepared using IFRS.

An annual report includes a full set of financial statements (income statement, balance sheet, statement of cash flows, and statement of shareholders' equity) and accompanying footnotes and describes the company's operations and financial conditions for the past year, which is provided annually to firm shareholders. Typically, an annual report also includes financial highlights, management's discussion and analysis along with the financial statements and accompanying footnotes, and an auditor's report. The SEC requires all publicly traded companies to provide this financial information; US public firms provide it via a form 10-K and non-US public firms via a form 20-F filed with the SEC. Currently, the forms are available directly from the SEC's website. Most firms also provide these data via their website. Technically, the 10-K/20-F and annual reports are different, although some companies provide their 10-Ks as their annual report on their websites.

MONSANTO/SYNGENTA

Monsanto (New York Stock Exchange stock symbol MON) and Syngenta (NYSE stock symbol SYT; Swiss Exchange (SWX) symbol SYNN) are two large public companies that operate in the 'agricultural chemicals' industry. They provide products for farmers including seeds, herbicides, and fertilizers that may be enhanced to assist in controlling the impact of insects, weeds, and bad weather on crops. Monsanto is domiciled in the US and Syngenta in Switzerland. The two companies are similar in size—Monsanto has about

22,000 employees with current annual revenues of about $11.4 billion, and Syngenta has about 21,000 full-time employees and reported revenues of about $10.8 billion last year. By comparing two very similar companies, we hope that differences across the two sets of financial reports would be more a function of the financial reporting process than differences in the companies themselves. Monsanto is included in the S&P 500, while Syngenta is included in the SMI (the Swiss Market Index—an index of the 20 largest and most liquid Swiss companies).

We begin with page 46 of the Monsanto annual report, where you will see 'Item 8. Financial Statements and Supplementary Data' at the top of the page. Monsanto uses its 10-K as its annual report and Item 8 refers to the order and specific information required by the SEC in its 10-K filing. Pages 46–49 include written declarations from Monsanto's management regarding their responsibilities for the financial statements and for internal control, and from the auditors regarding their assessment of Monsanto's internal controls and the outcome of their audit, respectively. The chief executive officer and the chief financial officer of Monsanto sign the first two declarations, as required by SOX, while the auditors sign the next two. These four declarations are relatively boilerplate declarations in part, because of the relatively strict requirements regarding what issues both management and the auditors must address in their statements. Similar declarations by Syngenta's management and auditors are included at the end of its report (pages 138–140). It is not subject to the same regulatory requirements as Monsanto. Syngenta does not provide a 'Management Report' although it does include a management report on internal control along with the auditors' report on both the financial statements and management's assessment of internal controls. Monsanto's pages 50–54 present the required four financial statements plus the Statements of Consolidated Comprehensive Income. Syngenta's pages 39–44 present the same information. In this case they use the titles 'income statement, balance sheet, cash flow statement, and statement of changes stockholders' equity' in that order.

Financial Statements

Income Statements

In their Statements of Consolidated Operations (page 50) and Consolidated Income Statements (page 30) Monsanto and Syngenta both present three years' worth of data – the current year and two previous years. Generally, US GAAP-prepared income statements have more specific categories listed than IFRS statements. US GAAP requires expenses to be presented based on function (e.g., cost of sales, administrative), while IFRS allows presentation based on function or nature (e.g., raw materials, staffing costs), which accounts for some of the differences. Ultimately, while there are differences between Monsanto's and Syngenta's income statements, they are similar in many respects. Both companies provide subtotals labeled 'Income from continuing operations' ($698 for Monsanto and $637 for Syngenta in 2006) and net income ($689 for Monsanto and $637 for Syngenta in 2006) as well as earnings per share for both continuing and discontinued operations.

Statement of Financial Position

Monsanto presents two years of data in its Statement of Consolidated Financial Position (page 51), while Syngenta's Consolidated Balance Sheet presents three years. Other than the number of years presented, the two balance sheets are structured very similarly. Assets and liabilities are listed from the most current to the least for both firms. However, this is frequently not the case when financial statements are prepared using IFRS. Often IFRS-prepared financial statements list assets and liabilities from the least current to the most current. For example, the first item listed on Fiat's balance sheet (an IFRS filer) is Intangible Assets, followed by Property, Plant, and Equipment. Cash and Cash Equivalents—the most liquid assets of all—are one of the last items listed in the Assets. In listing the 'other side' of the balance sheet, Fiat begins with stockholders' equity then moves on to long-term liabilities. Another commonly used method of presenting balance sheets entities is to present total assets less liabilities to obtain a 'net asset' amount, which then equals the total shareholders' equity. While neither IFRS nor US GAAP prescribes a format for the balance sheet, security market regulators may. Ultimately, the order in which the assets, liabilities, and stockholders' equity are listed in the balance sheet is a matter of convenience; we will label these types of differences as cosmetic. However, there are differences between US GAAP and IFRS that may initially appear to be cosmetic (e.g., including deferred taxes as noncurrent under IFRS and current under US GAAP), that, upon closer examination, have the ability to affect comparability across statements prepared using one set of standards and another. These differences may be more difficult to detect and, given their affect on comparability, will be labeled substantive and considered in more depth than cosmetic differences.

Statement of Cash Flows

Both Monsanto (page 52) and Syngenta (page 41) use the indirect method to present their information on the Statement of Consolidated Cash Flows. US GAAP and IFRS allow either the direct or indirect method, although the majority of firms elect to use the indirect method. The general structure across the two companies is similar; net cash flow from operating activities, investing activities, and financing activities are provided, as is the sum of those three and beginning and ending cash and cash equivalent amounts. You will discover that the classification of cash flows (among operating, financing, and investing) may differ between US GAAP and IFRS. Initially, this may seem to be a cosmetic difference, given the importance of ratios and other tools for analysis, these differences in classification will complicate comparing US GAAP and IFRS prepared financial reports.

Statement of Shareholders' Equity
Monsanto's Statements of Consolidated Shareholders' Equity (page 53) presents detailed information regarding changes in stockholders' equity accounts across the same periods presented in the income statement and statement of cash flows. Also included in Monsanto's financial statements is the Statements of Consolidated Comprehensive Income (page 54), which presents information about comprehensive income. US GAAP requires firms to "display total comprehensive income and its components" as part of a complete set of financial statements in one of three ways. Monsanto provides comprehensive income as a separate statement. (It is also permitted to provide this information as part of the income statement below net income or within the statement of stockholders' equity.) Syngenta presents its stockholder equity information in pages 42-44. Syngenta provides a separate section that details 'Gains and losses recognized directly in equity' within each year presented, similar to the information presented in Monsanto's Statements of Consolidated Comprehensive Income. These amounts are *not* included in net income, but do give rise to changes in the balance sheet from one period to the next. If the components related to 'recognized' income and expenses are provided separately, the statement is referred to as the SORIE (statement of recognized income and expenses). Similar to US GAAP, IFRS allows some flexibility in how comprehensive income information is presented. Differences between the presentation of stockholders' equity accounts under US GAAP and IFRS can be substantial. Complicating these differences in the presentation itself, are differences in terms used to identify specific items within the statement. One of the cosmetic differences between US GAAP- and IFRS-prepared financial reports is in the terminology allowed or employed. For example, it is quite common for IFRS-prepared financial statements to employ the term 'reserve' in labeling components of stockholders' equity, typically classified as part of retained earnings, including accumulated other comprehensive income, in US GAAP. In contrast, US GAAP filers are discouraged from using the term 'reserve' in their financial statements. As you gain familiarity with IFRS-prepared financial statements, you will find it easier to recognize differences in terminology that have no effect on comparability.

Footnotes
In addition to the actual financial statements, firms are required to provide a significant amount of information via footnote disclosures. Some of the disclosures are general in nature and provide information regarding overall

issues related to the preparation of the financial statements, while a significant number of them provide detailed information about specific accounts. The footnotes for Monsanto's financial statements encompass 39 pages—that's a *lot* of information! However, Syngenta's footnotes are 92 pages, more than twice the number of pages.

In both sets of footnotes, the first few footnotes provide general information regarding the company and preparation of its financial statements including how each accounts for typical transactions (e.g., revenue recognition issues) and information regarding how various assets and liabilities (e.g. accounts receivable, financial instruments, and environmental remediation liabilities) are recorded and valued. The remaining footnotes provide more detailed information, typically related to a specific account or accounts.

As noted on the financial statements, the 'accompanying notes are an integral part' of the consolidated financial statements. These notes provide additional details that either simply could not be included as part of the four statements themselves or would make them more difficult to read and comprehend. There are significant differences between US GAAP and IFRS in terms of required disclosures. While US GAAP requires substantial disclosures, IFRS tends to require even more. The role of at least some of this additional disclosure under IFRS is to provide users of financial reports with information that, under US GAAP, might be incorporated in the reported numbers. In short, many believe that US GAAP provides information through the application of rules and regulations in the reported outcomes along with footnotes. However, IFRS, which may not prescribe the 'correct' accounting for a given transaction, does require disclosures of more detailed information, to allow financial statement users to better understand the underlying transactions.

IFRS – US GAAP Reconciliation Footnote

One source of specific information regarding differences between IFRS- and US GAAP-prepared financial reports is a 'reconciliation' footnote found in the IFRS-prepared financial reports for firms that file form 20-F with the SEC. Prior to 2007 all foreign firms that listed on a US stock exchange and reported using any method of accounting other than US GAAP were required to provide, as a footnote in their annual (20-F) filing, a detailed reconciliation from the non-US GAAP earnings and stockholders' equity values to the values that would obtain if the firm had filed US GAAP. The information in this footnote is designed to assist US investors in translating non-US GAAP financial statements into values that they could better understand and use in making investment decisions (US GAAP). Typically, the reconciliation includes two tables that started with the non-US GAAP net income/stockholders' equity and ended with the US GAAP income/stockholders' equity. In between these values was a listing of specific items that differed between the two GAAPs. In addition to the tables, the reconciliation includes a narrative discussion of reconciling differences and additional disclosures required by US GAAP. Implicitly, the SEC-required reconciliation suggested that US investors were not required to understand non-US GAAP. These reconciliations provide a firm-specific direct measure of differences between US GAAP and IFRS; we will use them to help us better understand how and when those differences arise.

Syngenta's reconciliation is included in footnote 34 (of 36) and is 19 pages long (it starts on page 116 of the annual report). Based on this information, in 2006 Syngenta's net income under IFRS is $134 million greater than if US GAAP had been applied. In fact, IFRS net income is $1.33 ($0.66, $1.02) more *per share* than US GAAP net income. If we scale these differences by IFRS net income per share we can see that the decrease in net income in moving from the application of IFRS to the application of US GAAP is a relative change of between 10% and 23%! The same type of calculation can be made in comparing IFRS stockholders' equity and US GAAP stockholders' equity. In this case, we see that the total stockholders' equity reported under IFRS exceeds the US GAAP amount in 2006 by over $600 million. However, in prior years the difference flips or is relatively small. As we discuss the reasons for differences between US GAAP and IFRS reported values, we will consider when and why these differences may (or may not) be evident in stockholders' equity.

Within the reconciliations the firms provide a detailed list of the types of transactions that ultimately cause reported net income or stockholders' equity to differ. For example, within the net income reconciliation we see the purchase accounting related to Zeneca caused US GAAP income to exceed IFRS net income, while purchase accounting related to other transactions has the opposite impact. Two other items—pension provisions and grants of put options—significantly reduced IFRS net income relative to US GAAP values. A note references each line item within the reconciliation where detailed information about that line item is provided. (For example, the purchase accounting difference related to Zeneca refers to note a.) The 20-F footnote disclosures have provided a significant source of information to standard setters and others interested in differences between US GAAP and IFRS. They also provide salient examples of various types of differences to help us gain a better understanding of the US GAAP/IFRS differences in general.

US GAAP – IFRS Differences
While we all may agree that US GAAP-prepared financial reports present different values than IFRS-prepared reports, it is useful to have an overall sense of the magnitude and sign of those differences. Examining 20-F reconciliations from firms that disclosed differences between IFRS and US GAAP provides evidence of those differences, at least at a specific point in time. As discussed earlier, the reconciliation information was provided to the SEC who required that

non-US firms that were publicly traded on the US stock market reconcile these values to US GAAP through the 2006 reporting year. Therefore, this detailed information is only available for a small subset of publicly traded firms and will no longer be available after 2006.[2] In addition, firms clearly 'self-selected' into filing 20-Fs, so the reconciliations reflect differences based on a limited set of firms. Ultimately, calculated differences based on the 20-F reconciliations may not be generally comparable to what will be obtained in more current years or for all firms. It is also important to understand the volume and complexity involved in providing the reconciliation information. While it may be that differences between the two sets of standards can be condensed down to several pages in a financial report, the cost of maintaining the required information and preparing the information for stakeholder use is significant. In reality, companies were (virtually) required to maintain records based on applying both IFRS and US GAAP. Finally, many believe that US GAAP reporting results in 'transparent and high-quality' financial reports and question whether IFRS reporting will provide financial reports of equal quality. While reviewing the reconciliations does not allow us to address this concern directly, it does provide some insights into specific differences between financial reports based on the two sets of accounting standards for a subset of firms

Academic research based on information disclosed in 20-F reconciliations has examined several aspects of the filings. These studies document that, on average, earnings based on the application of IFRS exceeds earnings based on the application of US GAAP as often as 75% of the time. In contrast, however, the average *magnitude* of the difference in reported earnings when IFRS earnings exceed US GAAP earnings is about 25% (of the IFRS earnings), while the average magnitude of the difference in reported earnings when IFRS earnings are less than US GAAP earnings is about 70%. Similarly, stockholders' equity based on the application of IFRS exceeds earnings based on the application of US GAAP, although not as often as for reported earnings. The average magnitude of that difference when IFRS stockholders' equity exceeds US GAAP stockholders' equity is about 35% (of the IFRS stockholders' equity), while the average magnitude of the difference in reported stockholders' equity when IFRS stockholders' equity is less than US GAAP stockholders' equity is about 25%. While the magnitude of the differences for stockholders' equity is smaller than for earnings, it is important to remember that the scalar (denominator) is total stockholders' equity, a much larger value than current

---

[2] For firms that report based on the application of IFRS, the SEC eliminated the requirement for the reconciliation during 2007, so the 2006 reporting year is the last year for which this information is available from 20-F filings. Companies may elect to voluntarily provide this information to stakeholders. However, given the difficulty and cost of doing so, this is unlikely to happen.

year earnings; a 25% difference for earnings is not equivalent to a 25% difference for stockholders' equity.

Web Resources:
Securities and Exchange Commission – SEC – http://www.sec.gov/

CHAPTER 5:
CATEGORIZING DIFFERENCES

This section describes a method of categorizing specific differences between US GAAP and IFRS based on both reported outcomes and on underlying factors that cause those differences. Unlike many of the 'US GAAP—IFRS' updates, which systematically examine each accounting topic or type of transaction to identify when the two accounting systems require different reporting, we use an alternative approach that examines the differences from a broader perspective. We consider two dichotomies in reported outcomes that we label substantive/cosmetic and temporary/permanent. We also consider four fundamental factors within financial reporting (e.g., measurement, recognition threshold, classification, and rules) that are at work to obtain these differences. These dichotomies and factors will be instrumental in providing a framework for understanding and evaluating differences that arise between the two sets of accounting standards at a more general level. The benefit of this perspective is twofold. First, using a broader perspective, where differences are arranged based on some set categories scheme, simplifies the process of organizing and understanding this complex topic. The categories provides a mechanism to aid in understanding, rather than memorizing, differences in the application of US GAAP and IFRS. Second, a broader perspective will continue to be useful even as differences between US GAAP and IFRS change across time. As the FASB and IASB work towards convergence, differences between the sets of standards are not static but evolving. Given the rapid pace of change in both US GAAP and IFRS, these dichotomies and factors will have a longer-term benefit than memorizing specific differences that currently exist.

There are two issues to keep in mind as we discuss these categories and underlying factors. First, while they provide a structure to aid in understanding differences between US GAAP and IFRS, they are artificial and at some level arbitrary. We will rely on these dichotomies and factors in our discussions, but keep in mind that the purpose of doing so is to help you organize how you think about the two sets of standards. Second, the categories employed are not necessarily mutually exclusive. For example, we will classify the same transactions and accounts into substantive/cosmetic differences and temporary/permanent differences. In addition, the underlying factors can, and may, interact to cause a single difference in reported outcomes. For example, differences in pension accounting (that are substantive and have both temporary and permanent components) that give rise to different reported liabilities under US GAAP and IFRS may arise due to both measurement and recognition threshold differences.

TWO DICHOTOMIES

We use two dichotomous categories to organize differences in reported outcomes between US GAAP and IFRS: substantive/cosmetic and temporary/permanent.

Substantive/Cosmetic

Our first dichotomy separates differences in outcomes into those that are substantive in nature versus those that are cosmetic. Substantive differences are defined as those that arise when the application of US GAAP to a transaction provides an outcome or result that differs from IFRS *in substance*; the end result of the application of one set of standards versus another obtains a real difference that will ultimately affect comparability. In contrast, cosmetic differences arise when the application of US GAAP to a transaction provides an outcome or result that differs from IFRS, but in appearance or nonsubstantive ways only. Ultimately, substantive differences create the greatest difficulty in comparing financial reports prepared using US GAAP to those based on IFRS. Cosmetic differences, which may initially *appear* to significantly affect the financial reports, once identified should be relatively easy to deal with. This dichotomy should be most useful in assisting you in determining what differences truly matter. Cosmetic differences are relatively trivial to deal with, once identified. Figure them out and you can focus on differences that matter.

Temporary/Permanent

The second way to classify differences we consider is into those that are temporary and those that are permanent. Substantive differences that arise during one reporting period then reverse across time and ultimately go to zero can be considered temporary differences. Substantive differences that do not reverse, and thus continue to differ across time, are considered as permanent differences. In contrast to temporary differences, permanent differences are those whose effects will be ongoing and for which it will be difficult for investors to discern the continuing effects or know how to adjust for in comparing US GAAP and IFRS financial reports. Understanding whether, when, and how differences will or will not reverse will be very useful in assisting you in understanding how to translate between reported values based on US GAAP and reported values based on IFRS.

FOUR FUNDAMENTAL FACTORS

In concert with providing a categorization to sort differences in reporting outcomes between US GAAP and IFRS, we consider four underlying factors that may give rise to the differences. These four factors (measurement, recognition threshold, classification, and rules) focus on *why* differences arise in reported values or *how* or *where* those values are reported. The four factors will only be used to examine substantive differences, as they are much less usable or relevant for differences categorized as cosmetic. Below is a detailed description of each factor, including a discussion as to whether it tends to give rise to permanent or temporary differences.

Measurement

Measurement differences that arise between US GAAP- and IFRS-prepared financial reports arise because of differences in how specific items are measured (or valued) for each set of standards. In general, there are two ways in which measurement issues can cause differences between US GAAP and IFRS—due to differences in what measurement bases are applied or due to differences in the technical application of the same measurement base.

An example of when measurement differences arise due to different measurement bases can occur in the reporting of property, plant, and equipment (PPE). Firms that prepare financial reports using US GAAP use historical cost (purchase price) to value fixed assets, while those that use IFRS may elect to 'fair value' (assign value based on discounted expected future cash flows) to measure the value of PPE. If a firm chooses to use fair values for reporting the value of PPE, then the amount reported for the assets will differ based on which set of standards are adopted. These differences in reported values that arise between US GAAP and IFRS cause substantive differences, many of which are permanent. In the case of PPE, the underlying factor that gives rise to this reported difference between US GAAP and IFRS is the measurement bases that are allowed.

An example of when differences between US GAAP and IFRS arise due to the application of specific measurement techniques is when 'fair value' is employed under US GAAP versus IFRS. US GAAP obtains fair value measurements using exit price (the price received for selling an asset), while IFRS measures fair value as entry price (the price an asset would be bought for). While in many cases entry and exit values are the same, there are also a number of times when the price to buy a specific asset may differ from the selling price of that same asset. Consider a unique item, like a building designed and constructed for a firm, like Monsanto, to allow them to treat and process seed. If Monsanto needs to estimate the entry price, it will consider the cost to have the same building constructed or a similar physical location where it could treat and process seed, the cost of replacing the building (replacement cost). This value would likely need to consider the cost of rebuilding the current facility or of modifying some building to meet its needs. In contrast, if Monsanto were estimating the exit price, even without considering selling costs associated with the building, the estimated value would likely be very different than the value obtained for entry price. If Monsanto were to estimate the selling price of the building (net realizable value), it would have to incorporate into that value the fact that potential buyers may not find specific items included in the building (to make it suitable for Monsanto's needs) of any value to the potential buyer. In fact, some of those specific features may actually *reduce* the value of the building to users other than Monsanto. In short, the uniqueness of the asset in question often increases the difference between the replacement cost and the net realizable value. Clearly, defining fair value using exit prices in one set of standards versus entry value in the other set will result in substantive differences in reported values between US GAAP and IFRS. Measurement differences that arise due to differences in the technical application of a standard are typically permanent in nature.

Values obtained based on differences in measurement (e.g., historical cost, level 1 fair value, level 2 fair value) vary in reliability, one of the primary qualitative characteristics of information defined by both the FASB and IASB. Therefore, in situations where one set of standards selects a measurement technique that differs from the other set of standards, it may suggest that the boards are placing different 'weights' on relevance versus reliability in their decision. For example, consider when the IASB allows PPE to be revalued to fair value, while the FASB requires the use of historical cost. Many deem historical cost a more reliable measure of value than fair value (as historical cost is frequently more verifiable than fair value), while fair value is often considered more relevant than historical cost (particularly when an asset is held for a long period of time). In the valuing of PPE, it appears that the FASB has weighted the relative importance of relevance and reliability differently than the IASB or that the two boards differ in their beliefs regarding the reliability of fair value. As you consider differences between US GAAP and IFRS that are due to measurement, you may find it useful to try to gain a better understanding of whether the decision is based on relevance or reliability.

Generally, measurement-related differences are permanent in nature. If you consider the nature of measurement-related differences, where specific items are reported at values that differ based on the set of standards applied, you can see that these differences do not arise during one period of time and reverse in subsequent periods. As long as there is divergence in how the accounting standards determine and report the underlying value of an economic item, those differences will continue to exist across time.

Pause and Reflect: *The FASB and IASB have determined various ways to measure value within financial statements, including historical cost, fair value, and net realizable value. As you examine specific differences between US GAAP and IFRS that are due to measurement, consider why the boards might select different measurement bases to value the same items or why differences in technical applications occur. Select a specific difference between*

US GAAP and IFRS *due to measurement and analyze why this choice was made. Include in your analysis the inability to use specific measurement techniques in some settings and the tradeoff between relevance and reliability in determining which measurement model to apply.*

Recognition Threshold

There are situations where the source of differences between US GAAP and IFRS arise because of the point at which each set of standards consider that the item in question meets (or does not meet) some threshold to be considered as a given element. For example, recall the earlier discussion of development expenditures that, when applying IFRS, resulted in the formation of an asset, while under US GAAP the same expenditures were considered a current year expense. Under IFRS, the expenditure for development costs met a threshold to be recognized as an asset. However, under US GAAP, the board has determined this threshold for recognition has not been met. In this case, measurement is not an issue. The reported value of the transaction does not change. In one case the value is reported as an asset, which affects the balance sheet in the year of recognition and the income statement in future years, through amortization. In the other case, the value is reported as an expense the transaction is incurred. No asset is reported.

Recognition threshold-related differences frequently produce differences in whether reported items initially produce an asset/liability or expense/revenue. Ultimately, these differences 'shift' items across financial statements, typically from the balance sheet to the income statement (or vice versa). For example, expenditures for development costs that IFRS recognizes on the balance sheet will be 'shifted' to the income statement when US GAAP is applied. In addition, differences that arise due to recognition threshold are generally temporary, as they tend to arise in one year and reverse across subsequent years. As demonstrated in Chapter 1, this type of difference is typically reflected in both the reported asset/stockholders' equity values and reported income across a period of time, but eventually reverses. Given the frequency of this type of difference, their impact on both the income statement and balance sheet, and the importance of ratios based on the reported income statement and balance sheet numbers, understanding how and when recognition threshold differences exist will be important in comparing US GAAP and IFRS firms.

Classification

Substantive differences across financial reports prepared using US GAAP versus IFRS also arise due to classification. Classification-related fundamental factors are those that arise from differences in how one set of standards requires a transaction be classified versus the other set of standards. In contrast to recognition threshold-related factors, described above, classification differences tend to shift items from one category to another *within* a given financial statement, as when one set of standards requires classification as a liability while the other set may classify the same item as related to both liabilities and equity or when one set of standards reports an item in net income and the other reports it as part of other comprehensive income.

An example of a classification difference is in the reporting of compound financial instruments, like convertible bonds. Frequently, US GAAP requires this type of item be recorded as a liability. However, under IFRS the same compound instrument would be reported partially as a liability and partially as equity, based on the relative values of the bond portion and the conversion feature, where the value of the liability recorded under US GAAP will be allocated between debt and equity. As stakeholders view liabilities and equity very differently and the importance of debt versus equity on commonly used ratios (e.g., debt/equity; return on equity) is significantly different, the classification of a transaction as debt under one set of standards and as equity under the other can fundamentally affect the ability to compare US GAAP- and IFRS-prepared financial reports.

Another example of a classification difference between US GAAP and IFRS reporting is when an item is reported within the same financial statement and category, but 'shifted' within the category. For example, IFRS requires all deferred tax assets or liabilities to be classified as noncurrent, while US GAAP reports deferred taxes as current or noncurrent based on the related classification of the underlying asset or liability associated with the deferral or when the timing difference that gave rise to it will reverse. While a somewhat subtle difference, given the importance of ratios in assessing firm value and comparing across firms, this difference in classification can substantively affect how stakeholders view firms. Classification differences tend to be more permanent in nature than temporary, although some of them do reverse.

Rules

The fourth underlying factor we consider is related to whether the difference between US GAAP and IFRS is due to a specific rule. The issue of rules versus principles has been a topic of wide discussion as the use of IFRS has increased globally. This classification is unlike the others discussed earlier; it is based on what many consider a philosophical difference between US GAAP and IFRS. While some suggest that this philosophical difference is more a perception than a true difference, given the widespread perception and general level of interest in rules, we will incorporate it in our discussions and provide a more detailed discussion of this issue below.

Many suggest US GAAP is a 'rules-based' set of standards, while IFRS is considered a 'principles-based' set of standards. In fact, many infer that IFRS reliance on principles (or supposed lack of bright line rules) makes it a superior set of accounting standards relative to the rule-based US GAAP. Ostensibly, moving from a rules-based system toward a principles-based system will improve financial reporting, since a principles-based system will allow preparers and managers to exercise professional judgment which ultimately enhances transparency of financial statements and produces higher-quality reporting than a system that relies on a complex set of rules. However, in truth, both sets of standards are based on similar conceptual frameworks and both base the value of financial reports on the information's usefulness in decision making. Given the similar structures that underlie both sets of standards, it is reasonable to believe that the standards that arise would be equally similar.

Regardless of the underlying structure, the principles/rules issue is a widespread perception and one that concerns regulators, preparers, investors, and other stakeholders as the move towards IFRS is considered. In fact, many of the concerns raised are not really whether a 'rule' is adopted (i.e., the requirement to measure fair value using entry or exit value could be considered a rule) but really has to do with what are labeled 'bright lines' (an unambiguous set of criteria) in the application of standards. A frequently cited example of a bright line rule in is the accounting for leases. An firm may choose to enter into a leasing arrangement when acquiring assets for use in its business; the difficulty in accounting for leases arises when managers determine whether the lease is an operating lease (where the lease payments are expensed, but no asset or liability related to the lease is established) or a capital/financing lease (where an asset and liability are recorded along with interest and depreciation expense). While we will not list all the details, suffice it to say that the decision to classify a transaction as an operating or capital lease can be consequential in terms of both the balance sheet and the income statement.

Both US GAAP and IFRS state that the overriding issue considered in how to account for leased assets is whether "the risks and rewards" of ownership of the asset are transferred from the lessor to the lessee. If the risks and rewards are transferred, then accounting should reflect that transfer through a capital lease—the asset and corresponding liability should be transferred to the balance sheet. If not, then the asset remains on the lessor's books and the transaction is recorded as an operating lease. Under US GAAP, the classification decision rests completely on the details of the contractual arrangement between the lessee and the lessor, due to bright lines established in the specific standard. The standard states that, if the lease contract meets one of four specific rules (detailed in the standard), the transaction is considered a capital lease. If it does not meet these standards, then the lease is an operating lease. No professional judgment is required or allowed in making this decision. In contrast, IFRS includes no such 'bright line.' Instead, the standard establishes five criteria that are used to determine whether a lease is considered an operating or a financing lease.

The underlying concepts that determine whether a lease is operating or capital/financing are the same for both sets of standards (transfer of risks and rewards), but the specifics provided for application differ. For example, one of the four criteria that require a lease transaction to be accounted for as a capital lease under US GAAP states that "the lease term is equal to 75% or more of the estimated economic life of the leased property," establishing a strict value to determine whether the estimated economic life required for the transfer of risk and rewards happens. The standard is applied in very specific terms—firms can (and do!) structure leases so that the term of the lease is equal to just under 75% (like 74.5%) of the economic life, thereby avoiding the requirement to capitalize the lease. The issue of when the risk and rewards are transferred is considered under IFRS but no specific value is set to establish when that happens. Instead, judgment is required to determine whether the length of the lease meets the stated 'principle.' The difference between the two standards, which both rest on the concept of transfer of risks and rewards, is the numeric value provided in US GAAP, versus IFRS, which allows for judgment in that determination. In a case like this, the underlying factor that may cause a difference between US GAAP and IFRS is the application of a rule.

Many argue that the volume of US GAAP standards and guidance (which may exceed 30,000 pages of text) relative to the volume of IFRS standards and guidance (closer to 3,000 pages) is evidence of rules driving US GAAP relative to IFRS. Others argue that the difference is due to IFRS being 'immature' relative to US GAAP. In addition, many suggest that IFRS is less rule-oriented than US GAAP in part due to those that apply IFRS being able to rely on US GAAP when guidance is needed, diminishing the need for guidance under IFRS. In addition, the more recent proliferation of IFRS standards and guidance, as evidenced by the increase in the number of IFRS standards and interpretations, suggest that, across time and in response to pressure from auditors, preparers, and others, IFRS will become more rules-based. Finally, there are instances where the application of IFRS relies on specific guidance and US GAAP does not, inconsistent with IFRS being more principles-based than US GAAP. For example, the accounting for government grants is considered in IAS 20 and 41, while US GAAP does not provide specific accounting for such grants. There are also specific requirements under IFRS on how to present information related to insurance contracts, while no such guidance exists under US GAAP.

Ultimately, we could condense virtually all differences between US GAAP and IFRS into a rule. However, for our purposes, we will consider the three factors above before resorting to whether a rule causes the difference. The purpose of employing these factors is to provide a mechanism for organizing to help you better understand reporting differences between the application of US GAAP and IFRS. While 'rules' may not be as useful a factor as the other three in gaining an understanding, given the amount of discussion of this issue it is useful to understand the debate itself.

SUBSTANTIVE DIFFERENCES

Measurement related – US GAAP requires that property, plant and equipment be measured using historical cost less accumulated depreciation, while IFRS allows property, plant and equipment, to be revalued to fair value. Often PERMANENT.

Classification related – Generally, US GAAP requires that compound instruments, like convertible bonds, be recorded as a liability. Under IFRS a compound instrument must be separated into its debt and equity components, so the amount of liability recorded under US GAAP is allocated into part liability and part equity. Often PERMANENT.

Recognition threshold related – Generally, US GAAP expenses research and development costs (other than those related to software development costs) in the year incurred, as they do not meet the threshold to be considered an asset. However, IFRS allows development costs that are incurred once the technical and commercial feasibility of the asset for sale or use have been established to be capitalized and amortized instead of expensed. Often TEMPORARY.

Rules related – Both US GAAP and IFRS require that intangible assets be tested for impairment and that, if impaired, the value of that asset be written down to that amount. Under certain circumstances, IFRS allows the value of the asset to be written back up to historical cost, while US GAAP does not allow any impairment reversals. Often PERMANENT.

COSMETIC DIFFERENCES

Terminology related – Certain concepts in financial reporting are referred to using different terms in US GAAP than in IFRS. Examples of these differences include, the use of plan versus scheme (e.g., referring to a pension *plan* in US GAAP as a pension *scheme* in IFRS) and the use of capital versus financing (e.g., referring to a *capital* lease in US GAAP as a *financing* lease in IFRS).

Placement related – The overall organization of the financial statements may differ between US GAAP-prepared financial statements and IFRS-prepared financial statements. For example, US GAAP balance sheets list assets and liabilities from the most current items to the least current. However, IFRS-prepared financial statements may or may not list the most current items first. Frequently, the order is reversed, where long term assets (e.g., goodwill or property, plant, and equipment) are the first assets listed on the balance sheet for IFRS statements instead of cash and cash equivalents as is provided by US GAAP-prepared statements. In addition, a US GAAP balance sheet will present total assets as equal to total liabilities plus stockholders' equity, while some IFRS-prepared statements will present net assets (total assets less total liabilities) as equal to stockholders' equity.

APPLYING THE DICHOTOMIES AND FACTORS

Now that we have defined the dichotomies and factors, let's see how we might apply them in gaining a better understanding of a difference between US GAAP and IFRS reported values. If you take a look at the Syngenta 20-F reconciling footnote referenced earlier, you will see that the third "US GAAP adjustment" listed is related to restructuring charges. In 2006 and 2005, the effect of accounting for restructuring charges under IFRS versus accounting for the same transaction after applying US GAAP was to reduce IFRS net income (of $634 million) by $9 million. In other words, if US GAAP standards had been applied the expense associated with restructuring charges would have exceeded the amount actually recorded by Syngenta when it applied IFRS by $9 million. In 2004 the effect would have been reversed and much larger—restructuring charges under US GAAP would have been $47 million *less than* the amount recorded by Syngenta.

Technically (based on reading footnote c included in the reconciliation footnote), we can see that this difference arises as follows: when reporting restructuring charges, IFRS require companies to estimate costs associated with the restructuring and charge them against income in the year a formal plan to restructure is made and, if those costs have not yet been paid out, set up a liability for the unpaid costs. In contrast, US GAAP does not allow companies to charge costs associated with restructuring against income or establish a liability until the actual event that produces the costs arise. In this specific case, estimated costs associated with the restructuring (including costs of terminating employees who were to be eliminated during the restructuring) were charged to net income, along with a corresponding liability, in the year the plans were initiated under IFRS in 2004. However, since the event that actually gave rise to the costs (the termination of the employees) did not take place in 2004, those costs were not expensed in that year under US GAAP, but instead were expensed in subsequent years when the actual terminations took place. Ultimately, under IFRS, some restructuring expenses that were accrued during 2004 were not allowed as an expense for US GAAP purposes at that point in time. Similarly, no liability for unpaid costs was established. Instead, those expenses would be recorded as they are incurred in future years (2005 and 2006, etc.). So, how does this series of transactions fit into our more theoretical view of things?

The difference between US GAAP and IFRS reported income caused by restructuring charges is a substantive one—an expense and a liability within a financial report prepared under one set of standards has one value but that same expense and liability would be a different value if the financial report had been prepared using the other set of accounting standards. In addition, from our discussion, we can see that this difference between US GAAP and IFRS is a temporary one. Across time, as Syngenta completes its restructuring, the total expenses associated with it will be the same, regardless of the set of accounting standards applied. If you were to track this reconciling item across time, you would see that the sum of the restructuring reconciling items that increase net income would be equal to the sum of the restructuring reconciling items that decrease net income; therefore, the cumulation of the total restructuring reconciling items would eventually reconcile to zero. Economically, the application of one set of accounting standards over another does not change the restructuring costs but simply changes the financial reporting period when that cost affects the reported net income.

The above discussion describes how this substantive difference arises, but *why* does this happen? The technical details suggest that the origin of the difference is due to the factor we label recognition threshold: based on standards established by the IASB (IFRS) the threshold to record a restructuring expense and a liability has been met at the time that a formal plan is made, while under US GAAP that threshold is not met until the expenditures have been made.

CONCLUSION

The type of analysis above, examining a specific transaction to determine what type of difference is generated and which factor(s) causes that difference, condenses a relatively complex series of transactions into a more straightforward general understanding of this difference. It will allow you to better begin the process of understanding differences in reported earnings under IFRS captures the economic earnings. A line-by-line comparison of financial reports prepared under US GAAP versus those prepared under IFRS would reveal a number of differences between the set of reports. As an aid to organizing and understanding these differences, we will sort specific differences into two classifications (substantive/cosmetic and temporary/permanent) and four fundamental factors (measurement, recognition threshold, classification, and rules). While somewhat arbitrary and overlapping, these classifications will allow us to better understand and consider the underlying factors that drive the reporting differences.

CHAPTER 6:
US GAAP AND IFRS—SOME DIFFERENCES

There are a large number of differences between financial reports prepared after applying US GAAP and those based on IFRS. Several of these have been discussed as examples in the earlier chapters and, if you have spent any time researching IFRS, you have probably heard about a number of others. In this chapter, we highlight several differences between US GAAP and IFRS beyond those discussed in earlier chapters and provide you with a general explanation of the technical differences all within the framework discussed in Chapter 5. This analysis should prove useful to you by increasing your familiarity with the system we outline and how it might be linked with some of the more technical aspects of the differences between the sets of accounting standards. In addition, the general areas that we present below (e.g., consolidations, inventory) were selected based on their importance (in terms of frequency or magnitude) in generating differences between the two sets of standards. However, a caveat! Given the brevity of this supplement, the plethora of differences between US GAAP and IFRS, and the rapid changes in both sets of standards (which changes the differences between them), do not rely on these materials alone in your assessment of differences between US GAAP and IFRS.

SPECIFIC DIFFERENCES

Below we discuss areas where significant differences continue to be observed between US GAAP- and IFRS-prepared financial reports. In light of space and time limitations, we present a brief discussion of some items and a more in-depth discussion of others. While this list is far from comprehensive, it should provide you with a starting point in understanding differences and how to use the classification system to help you understand them and how you might adjust or consider financial reports prepared under the two systems to make them more comparable. As you read through the discussions below, you may note that in some cases the discussion is presented in terms of a broader issue (e.g. consolidation or impairment), while in other cases the discussion is related to a specific account or type of account (e.g., inventory or financial instruments). We want to highlight this fact, so you can use it as you consider differences between US GAAP and IFRS—it just seemed the best way to organize the more specific discussions. However, do recognize that the broader issue discussions can, and do, relate to a number of accounts.

Consolidation

When preparing consolidated financial statements, there still exist significant differences between the two sets of standards, including the determination of when entities will be consolidated with the parent. In making that determination both sets of standards rely on the issue of control. However, US GAAP bases control on a controlling financial interest model, while IFRS bases it on control in terms of governance and risks and rewards. While it is beyond the scope of this discussion to go into specific details, there are differences in when control is considered obtained. To further complicate the issue, some terms/concepts that are found in US GAAP related to consolidated entities (e.g. variable interest entity (VIE) and qualified special purpose entity (QSPE)) are not found within IFRS. Thus, when US GAAP requires specific determination of control based on whether the potentially consolidated subsidiary is a VIE or QSPE, IFRS treats these entities as simply subsidiaries.

Simply put, the entities included within a consolidated statement tend to be broader under IFRS than US GAAP. Under IFRS, which focuses on a model of risks and rewards when control is not evident (in terms of ownership of more than 50%), more subsidiaries are consolidated than under US GAAP, where the determination of control is based first on a variables interests model and then on voting control. In addition, under US GAAP there exists specific guidance (typically industry level) where consolidation is not required.[3]

Given the brief discussion above, how do we fit differences based on consolidation-related issues in our classification system? To begin, the differences between reporting under one system and another are substantive; reported values will differ and they will be permanent. The underlying factor that causes this difference could be considered, in a broad sense, an issue of recognition threshold. The two sets of standards set different thresholds in determining when the concept of 'control' is met.

Impairment of Long-lived Assets

Another significant area of differences between US GAAP and IFRS is in terms of the issue of impairments. This area has the potential to cause significant substantive differences in reported values between US GAAP and IFRS that tend to be permanent in nature. Furthermore, impairment issues can affect most of the long-lived assets carried on the balance sheet; this discussion is included to provide an understanding of the issue related to all long-lived financial and nonfinancial assets (e.g., property, plant, and equipment, intangible assets).

---

[3] US GAAP is undergoing significant changes toward converging with IFRS in this area (see FAS 160, effective for years beginning on or after December 31, 2008). Included in this standard is a requirement that minority interest (noncontrolling interest) be included as part of equity, not within the mezzanine or as a liability, consistent with IFRS.

Impairment is based on an assessment of whether the value of an asset has suffered an 'other than temporary' decline in value, suggesting the need to write the asset down to its impaired value. Issues of impairment arise for all types of assets—those that are depreciated (property, plant, and equipment), those that are fair-valued (inventory), and those that may or may not be subject to amortization (software development costs or goodwill). There are three ways that we might obtain significant differences between US GAAP and IFRS in reported values related to impairments. The first is in the determination of whether impairment has actually occurred and the second is related to the calculation of the impaired value. The third issue is related to the ability to reverse an impairment charge, which is generally (but not perfectly descriptive) 'yes' for IFRS and 'no' for US GAAP. We discuss each of these issues below. Given the differences in the standards relative to financial and nonfinancial assets, we will consider each type of asset individually.

Financial Assets
Differences in the impairment of financial assets under US GAAP and IFRS are partially a function of the type of financial asset. Below we consider the accounting for held-to-maturity (HTM) debt securities and how the two sets of standards vary in determining if an impairment occurs, in the method of measuring the impaired value, and whether the impairment can be reversed.

Determining whether an impairment of debt securities (securities carried at amortized cost) has occurred under US GAAP varies with the entity's 'intent' and its ability to hold the security, consistent with the classifications into AFS and HTM reflected in the accounting at acquisition. Under US GAAP several issues are considered to determine whether an 'other than temporary' decline in value has occurred, including the entity's ability and intent to hold the security until it can recover, the length of time that the market value has been below historical cost, and changes in market interest rates. In contrast, IFRS focuses on 'trigger events' that affect the recovery of the cash flows from the security without considering intent. IFRS considers 'objective evidence' (e.g., the significant financial difficulty or high probability of bankruptcy of the issuer or a breach of contract or delinquency) along with whether that event has an expected impact on the expected future cash flows in its determination of an impairment. These differences between the standards reflect different thresholds at which each recognizes an impairment.

In determining the means of measuring the impaired value of the security, the two sets of standards differ as well. Under US GAAP the impaired value is measured as the fair market value of the security (the discounted present value of the future expected cash flows). In contrast, IFRS measures the impaired value of HTM securities as the discounted present value of the currently estimated amounts and timings of payments, using the *original* effective interest rate. If the original effective interest rate differs from the current effective interest rate, then the IFRS measured value may not equal the fair market value used under US GAAP.

Consistent with most of US GAAP, impairment losses for HTM debt securities are prohibited—the impaired value establishes a new cost basis for the investment that cannot be written up. In contrast, IFRS allows the impairment loss to be reversed if there is objective evidence than an event occurred that reduced the loss after the impairment date. This reversal is limited to what would have been the original amortized cost.

In summary, in the accounting for impairments related to debt securities, differences between the sets of standards in determining if an impairment has occurred is due to recognition threshold differences, in determining the impaired value differences are due to measurement issues, and in the ability to reverse the impairment differences are due to a rule.

Pause and Reflect. *Consider how impairments of available-for-sale equity securities under US GAAP and IFRS differ using the structure applied in the discussion of 'held-to-maturity debt securities' above. Analyze the differences related to when each set of standards determines an impairment has occurred, how the calculated values are determined, and whether the impairment can or cannot be reversed. Determine which of the four fundamental factors are related to the determination, valuation, and reversal. Consider the usefulness of the classification system in generalizing how US GAAP and IFRS tend to account for these types of assets.*

Nonfinancial Assets
There are differences in the required testing for potential impairments between US GAAP and IFRS, which may lead to recognition of an impairment under IFRS when US GAAP would require no such recognition. Basically, US GAAP requires a two-step process, where the first step is used to determine whether an impairment has occurred and the second step calculates the fair (impaired) value. In the first step, the sum of the undiscounted expected cash flows to be received from the asset are compared to the carrying value to determine if the impairment has occurred. If so, the impaired value is calculated as the fair value (exit price) of the asset. In contrast, IFRS skips the first step and simply calculates the recoverable amount (either fair value less costs to sell or the sum of the *discounted* expected cash flows to be received from the asset) as its potentially impaired value. If this recoverable amount is less than the carrying value, then an impairment has occurred. This difference in determining if and when impairment has actually occurred is the first source of differences between US GAAP and IFRS. This difference in the testing for the potential impairment of long-lived assets held for use may lead to earlier impairment recognition under IFRS. We classify this difference as one caused by differences in recognition threshold under US GAAP and IFRS.

The second way that impairments may cause differences between reported US GAAP and IFRS values is in the actual calculation of the impaired value, once it has been determined that an impairment exists. As stated earlier, in the second step of its two-step process, US GAAP calculates the impaired value as the fair value of the asset, or the exit price. However, IFRS bases its impaired value on the recoverable amount, which may (or may not) end up being the same value obtained for exit price from US GAAP. Thus, if an impairment is established under both sets of standards, this difference between US GAAP and IFRS is due to measurement, where one set of standards measures the impaired value using one measurement technique and the other another way.

The third way in which impairments may cause a difference in reported values between the two sets of standards is due to a difference in whether each set of standards allows for a reversal of an impairment charge. US GAAP does not allow reversals of any impairments of long-term fixed assets, while IFRS allows for such reversals for all long-term assets except for goodwill. However, that reversal is limited to the amount that was originally written off when the asset was considered impaired. In other words, IFRS requires an asset to be written down (impaired), if need be. If conditions warrant, it also allows an asset to be written back up to the original cost. This ability to write assets up as well as down under the impairment standard means that the reported value of assets under IFRS is more variable than under US GAAP. Given the nature of the difference between the two sets of standards, we classify this difference as arising due to a rule.

In summary, differences in the impairment standards between US GAAP and IFRS may result in substantive, permanent differences between values reported under the two systems. The underlying factors that cause these differences include the recognition threshold (differences in determining if an impairment exists), measurement (differences in the measurement bases used to measure the value of the impaired asset), and rules (US GAAP prohibits the reversal of impairments while IFRS does not). Each of these factors needs to be considered in understanding issues related to accounting for impairments.

Inventory

Inventory accounting is an area where differences still exist between the values reported under US GAAP and IFRS. In general, there are three ways in which the accounting for inventory tends to differ. The first of these is related to the inventory costing or flow assumption applied. US GAAP allows the use of LIFO (last-in, first-out), which is not allowed under IFRS. In addition, under IFRS entities are required to use the same 'cost formula' (e.g., FIFO (first-in, first-out)) for all 'similar' inventories, which is not required under US GAAP. The prohibition against the use of LIFO in IFRS has the potential to have a significant impact on reported operating results as well as on current income taxes payable, given the book/tax LIFO Internal Revenue Service conformity rules.[4] The second area where US GAAP and IFRS differ is in how inventory is valued. US GAAP requires the use of 'lower of cost or market,' whereas under IFRS inventory is to be carried at 'lower of cost or net realizable value.' US GAAP defines market as the replacement cost, as long as it is greater than net realizable value (estimated selling price less reasonable costs of completion and sale) and less than net realizable value less a normal sales margin. If replacement cost is greater than both of these, then market value is defined as net realizable value. If it is less than both, then it is defined as net realizable value less a normal sales margin. IFRS defines net realizable value as the best estimate of the amounts inventories are expected to realize. Based on these definitions, it may be that inventory that is valued as the 'market' in the lower of cost or market approach under US GAAP will not be valued the same as the 'net realizable value' obtained under IFRS. The third way that US GAAP and IFRS inventory accounting differs has to do with the reversal of write-downs of inventory due to impairments, discussed in the earlier section on impairments.

In summary, differences between inventory-related accounting based on the application of US GAAP and IFRS have the potential to differ due to rules (the ability to use LIFO, the requirement to use the same costing assumptions for all similar inventory, and the impairment reversal issue) as well as due to measurement differences (the use of market value versus net realizable value). Now that you better understand the circumstances when specific issues arise, you should be better able to distinguish among these differences and the resulting expected impact on comparability. For example, if you are evaluating issues related to an inventory write-down to lower of cost or market (or net realizable value), you know you will need to consider whether the value presented in the financial report might differ if the alternative set of standards were applied.

An interesting note related to the issue of convergence. The accounting for inventory and differences between that accounting based on the two sets of standards was recently addressed, resulting in part in IFRS 2. While there are still differences between the two sets of standards (as discussed above), there are no current projects underway by the board or boards to deal with those differences. The fact that significant differences still exist, even after efforts by both boards towards minimizing those differences on this specific issue, suggests that the path toward complete convergence is not yet clear.

Financial Instruments

Accounting for financial instruments under either set of standards is highly complex and explaining the underlying accounting under each set of standards and the differences between them in detail is well beyond the scope of this text.

---

[4] The Internal Revenue Service requires firms that use LIFO for tax purposes do so for financial reporting purposes as well. If firms are required to change to another inventory costing system it has the potential in increase reported income and, therefore, current income taxes payable.

Nonetheless, that does not mean that you cannot gain a general level of understanding of the differences between the standards using the classification system devised earlier. However, instead of discussing the differences and then considering the causes of them as we have done earlier, this time we will consider each of the causes and discuss specific issues related to financial instruments that fall within each category. Again, our discussion is not all-inclusive, but is designed to provide you with tools to assist you as you learn more about IFRS.

Measurement
As stated earlier, measurement issues are fundamentally tied to two items—the measurement bases allowed or required by each set of accounting standards or differences in the technical application of the same measurement bases. Both of these measurement issues are found within accounting for financial instruments under US GAAP versus IFRS and have the potential to give rise to significant differences in reported values, both on the balance sheet and in the income statement.

Fair value measurements are probably most widely used in accounting for financial instruments than in any other area within both US GAAP and IFRS. While relatively the same in theory across US GAAP and IFRS, the FASB and the IASB have decided the practical application of fair value differs. Fair value calculated under US GAAP is based on the exit price, while fair value calculated under IFRS is based on entry price. We have discussed this issue at length in an earlier chapter, so we will not repeat it here.

Recognition Threshold
Differences between financial reports prepared under US GAAP and IFRS that we attribute to recognition threshold arise because of the point at which each set of standards consider the item in question to have met some threshold to be considered an element in financial reporting. This factor typically shifts the recognition of an element from one statement (e.g., the income statement) to another (e.g., the balance sheet). Previously, we considered differences in the recording of expenditures related to development costs, where US GAAP expensed the costs in the current period and IFRS established an asset that was amortized across time, as an example of recognition threshold.

The recognition threshold factor could also be considered when assessing how US GAAP and IFRS derecognize financial assets. In the case of derecognition issues, the question that arises is whether the transfer of an asset qualifies for removing that asset from the entity's balance sheet. IFRS evaluates whether a transfer of a financial asset qualifies for derecognition by considering whether substantive risks and rewards (and in certain cases, control), are transferred. In contrast, under US GAAP derecognition focuses on the loss of control over the transferred assets based on specific conditions without explicit consideration of the risks and rewards. Instead legal, actual, and effective control is assessed to determine derecognition. Ultimately, because of differences in derecognition thresholds, derecognition, (e.g., off-balance-sheet treatment of asset securitization transactions) will be less frequent under IFRS.

Classification

We consider classification differences as those that tend to shift reported items from one category to another *within* a given financial statement. Differences in the classification of financial assets across the two sets of standards can be particularly consequential, as the classification of financial assets can affect the measurement of them. For example, under US GAAP, the value of a debt security that is classified as a trading security is measured using fair market value while the exact same asset, if classified as HTM, would be measured using amortized cost.

One example of significant classification differences between US GAAP and IFRS is in the classification of financial assets in general. IFRS requires that financial assets be classified in one of four categories: held for trading (requiring measurement at fair value with changes in fair value reported in earnings), AFS (requiring measurement at fair value with changes in fair value reported in comprehensive income), HTM investments (requiring measurement at amortized costs), and loans and receivables (which may be classified as trading, AFS, or HTM). In contrast, US GAAP has several standards and related guidance to establish the classification of financial assets. Two examples of differences in classification (and the related measurement of those assets) include loans and receivables and unlisted equity securities. Under US GAAP loans and receivables may be classified as held for sale and measured as the lower of cost or market, an option unavailable under IFRS. Similarly, under US GAAP unlisted equity securities are scoped out of the classification of trading, AFS, and HTM, and are measured at cost, while IFRS requires equity instruments be measured at fair value, if reliably measurable.

Rules

The final of the four factors is related to specific rules, including industry-specific guidance, that result in different reported outcomes between US GAAP and IFRS. An example of this type of guidance related to financial assets pertains to the accounting for unlisted equity securities. US GAAP accounting for these assets by general corporate entities that do not choose the fair value option (carried at cost), for example, differs significantly from accounting for these assets by broker/dealers, investment companies, and insurance companies, who are required to carry these assets at fair value. In contrast, the accounting for unlisted equity securities under IFRS is the same regardless of the industry in which the entity in question operates.

In summary, we are able to analyze the four factors that cause differences between US GAAP and IFRS reported values as they relate to the reporting of financial assets. While an extremely complex area of financial reporting, we see that classifying the differences between the two sets of standards in terms of the four factors can prove useful in presenting a summary of expected differences or areas of limited comparability between reported values under US GAAP versus IFRS. For example, we can see that classification differences are an important consideration in explaining potential differences and how specific financial assets are measured.

CONCLUSION

In this chapter we provide specific details where differences between US GAAP and IFRS obtain different reported values. In our discussions, we focus on the general reporting issues related to the accounting outcomes, with a focus on understanding how our four classifications (measurement, recognition threshold, classification, and rules) can be used to categorize the differences that arise in the accounting. Many of the accounting issues that we discuss are related to technical issues that are relatively complex, which may deter you from gaining or attempting to gain an understanding of how financial reports based on US GAAP differ from reports based on IFRS (or vice versa). However, taking a broader, theoretical perspective to view the differences provides a means of gaining a better understanding of comparability and potential differences that may be difficult to gain by a focus on technical differences alone. We encourage you to apply your understanding of the fundamental ways in which US GAAP and IFRS can and do differ as you continue to discuss and learn about the two sets of standards.